Poems *from the* Asylum

Martha H. Nasch

The terms "hospital," "institution," and "asylum" are used interchangeably throughout this anthology. Though each term carries a connotation of more positive or negative living conditions (alternatively, "treatments," "confinement," or "imprisonment"), the editorial team remains decidedly uncommitted to a singular opinion and defers to the original author's eyewitness account for further exploration.

Editor/Publisher: J. Molony
Cover Design and Interior: J. Molony
Cover Image: Martha Nasch wedding portrait, 1913. (Courtesy Ralph Nasch)
Web: www.JanelleMolony.com
Social Media: www.Facebook.com/SevenYearsInsane

ISBN: 978-1-7344638-4-2 (HB)
ISBN: 978-1-7344638-5-9 (PB ltd.)
Non-Fiction Reference Book / Poetry Anthology
Genres: Poetry, Mental Health
Keywords: Ramsey County, Minnesota, Asylum, Genealogy

Reviews for *Poems from the Asylum*

"*Poems from the Asylum* is a true honor to Martha's life and legacy. So many people tried to break her ... but she was a master old soul with a fighting spirit. Writing poetry saved her sanity."

Michelle A. Cox-Lomas, Ph.D.,
Psychologist & Case Study Consultant, Michigan

"A satisfactory read ... for historians, poetry lovers, [and] mental health workers."

Beth Zabel, Volunteer Services Coordinator,
St. Peter State Hospital Museum, Minnesota

"*Martha's story* restores dignity and self-respect ... to so many women diagnosed with a mental illness."

Mary Ann Lancette Palumbo,
St. Paul Historian, Minnesota

Poems *from the* Asylum

Martha H. Nasch

Edited & Arranged by Janelle Molony, M.S.L.

Introduction by Jodi Nasch Decker, Ed.D.

Dedication

Dear Emma: I have written a book of poetry for you, which I have composed as a memory. Let me know if you get this book. 1932.

—Martha Gruening Nasch

Preface

As the senior editor of Martha Nasch's poems, I have critically evaluated each with regard to mechanical form, signature habits, and standard conventions to learn her voice. With this in mind, I have made minor modifications to assist modern readers with comprehension, particularly regarding punctuation and layout. Misspellings were considered as either errors, invented words, or conventional and appropriate to the era and education level of the original author. Original spellings are maintained when they do not create confusion and are indicated with italics. I have also taken the liberty of re-ordering the poems into thematic groupings for the reader's convenience. The original order in which the poems appeared in Martha's asylum notebook is included in the Appendix. Even with these adjustments, there have been no compromising changes to Martha's words or the spirit and intention behind them (for better or for worse).

As an additional reader's aid, three specific metaphors repeatedly used by Martha are defined here:

1.   An empty or vacant chair (to indicate a person missing from life),

2.   A door (as an entry into a relationship, or exit from one), and

3.   A shore (as the boundary between life and death, or the afterlife).

Finally, please keep in mind that while the majority of Martha's poems are homesick or reflective in nature, many contain disturbing and violent ideas which are not suitable to a young reader or listener audience. Please use discretion when discussing or presenting the material.

Respectfully, Janelle Molony

Acknowledgments

I owe a debt of appreciation to several individuals and organizations who provided access to a treasure trove of historical information and photographs that made publishing this authoritative book possible:

Jodi Nasch Decker, Mary Ann Palumbo, MaryAnn Elias Johnson, Karen Hogendorf, Lisa Boelke, Cindy Keis Mitsch, Debbie Kammerer, Dr. P. Leslie Herold, Dr. Michelle Cox-Lomas, Denise Clark, Lori Sudgen, Katie Paulson, Melodee Beckman, Art Paape, Bruce Linz, Logan L. Hurst, Beth Zabel, Jane Haala, Minnesota Historical Society, Ramsey County Historical Society, Nicollet County Historical Society, and the St. Peter State Hospital Museum.

Thank you, again, Janelle Molony

Contents

Poems Dated 1928–1932

III: Our Child, A Pawn

IV: So, Here I Rot

Introduction

Martha Hedwig Nasch

Jodi Nasch Decker, Ed.D.

Granddaughter of Martha Nasch

1

Illustration 1: Ralph L. Nasch (18) graduated from Humboldt High School on June 14, 1940. Parents, Martha (50) and Louis (56), Nasch would divorce the following year.

Credit: Unknown photographer. Courtesy of Ralph Nasch.

My father, Ralph Louis Nasch (1921-2019), would tell me very few details about his mother, Martha Hedwig Nasch (1890-1970). He shared even less when it came to discussing her stint in an insane asylum during the Depression Era. "As you may recall," he'd written to me when I pressed him for more information, "my mother was in the State Hospital in St. Peter for about six years, between my ages of six and twelve. She was very irrational at times, frequently believing the devil was out to get her. When she was clear minded, she wrote poetry that was very good but it dealt mostly with her miseries, unhappiness, and misfortunes in life" (Ralph Nasch, 1998).

After the passing of my mother, Marie Frances Nasch (1927-2011), the loss reminded me that not only do we no longer have a person's physical body near when they die, but we also lose their words, stories, memories and wisdom. The fresh wound of a parental loss gave me courage to re-approach the subject of my grandmother with my father once more. I could not take any memories for granted anymore. So, we, my daughter and I, began to explore what had previously been a dark family secret to try and bring it to light with a fresh perspective.

"I seem to recall that she attempted suicide once or twice but was unsuccessful," my father explained further, but we couldn't figure out whether those were before or during her institutionalization (Nasch, 1998). In a notebook of Martha's poetry given to me by my father, my grandmother suggests suicide by hanging or by a steep fall as ways to escape the trauma she'd experienced in her thirties. She also includes in her poetry several life-ending options for Louis Jacob Nasch Jr., her then-husband and my grandfather, to consider. Through ongoing family history research, I'd learned my grandparents' romance had soured long before Martha documented her woes.

Louis Jr. also preserved his own version of the Nasch family history in extensive letters detailing the minutiae of important family member origins, significant dates, and other personal recollections that he passed along to my father in the 1950s and 60s. In addition to this, my father elaborated on his childhood experience in a lengthy reminiscence, now in my possession. Between the three individuals who could ever know the truth about my grandmother's asylum committal, the answers I sought were evasive. Why the great secrecy?

In one of Louis Jr.'s family history accounts, he wrote to his son, "You were then six years, two months, twelve days old on the day mother left" (1963). He afforded no explanation beyond the date of Martha's hospital admission. His choice of words suggests Martha was (to a degree) willing to be admitted to the hospital or in some way responsible for her extended absence.

In today's vernacular, my father would be referred to as a "latch-key kid" while his mother was in the St. Peter State Hospital for the Insane. He said to me, "I was alone much of the time when [Louis] was working. He told me to go to the neighbor's next door if I had a need or a problem. We had no telephone until I was a teenager and many evenings, I would be alone, waiting for him to come home from work until six or six-thirty p.m. I often wondered what would happen to me if he died or became incapacitated" (1998).

My grandfather, Louis Jr., and father, Ralph, made it a priority to visit my grandmother in the hospital every two weeks, on Sundays. Since Louis Jr. had no vehicle, this required a two-hour, one-way bus ride from St. Paul, Minnesota. My father does not recall a time when Martha ever came home, though it is impossible to say if a temporary release was even an option for her during her time of treatment.

Being the child of a mentally ill mother made my father feel deeply ashamed and embarrassed, even as an adult. Growing up, for him at least, the subject of mental illness was not a culturally acceptable topic to openly acknowledge, and more so, not one a person would readily admit to due to the potential for taunting. Sometimes, when I pressed my father for more details about my grandmother, he would tell me he didn't remember anything new, or laugh awkwardly and say it wasn't interesting. It always felt like that response was supposed to end the discussion. I never quite understood his depth of shame until we dug deeper into the past. First, we researched covertly, trying not to upset him. Then, only when we learned more about the precipitating factors for her commitment, did he warm up to the conversation again.

To clarify, I didn't know my grandmother well. We lived in different states, and she never traveled to visit us. We drove form out of state to visit her. I didn't understand why as a kid, but later learned from my father, "she never had too much interest in the grandchildren" (1987). There are some revealing photos of her holding me as an infant, but her facial expression is not one of an adoring grandmother, happy to see the newest family addition. Instead, she is peering intently at me, as if I were a science experiment.

One particular memory I have of visiting my grandmother, Martha Nasch, stands out beyond all others. I may have only been eight or nine years old when my mother, Marie, brought me with her to visit in the late 1960s. Martha was senile at the time, and she and her second husband were in an assisted living home in Gaylord, Minnesota, a short drive south of St. Paul. She definitely had no idea who I was at the visit, and I am not so sure she even recognized my mother. I sincerely wish that the hospital staff had warned us about her state of mind before we walked into that room.

She screeched from her hospital bed, "The devil is coming to get me!" It was terrifying for me. My father heavily downplayed these events in his descriptions. He wrote, "She had some strange hallucinations … that played havoc with her mind and tortured her" (1987).

She was a specter of a woman with wild and thinning white hair, in a flimsy standard-issue hospital gown that fluttered around her when she'd moan and shake. At nearly eighty years old, she seemed to be in the worst physical agony and spiritual torture of her life. Over and over, she proclaimed the devil was coming to take her away and that she saw demons crawling up the walls. This frightening encounter has haunted me ever since.

No child should be so horrified to visit their grandmother. In retrospect, I can only speculate if this was the expression of a latent mental illness or if she was struggling in the later stages of what we now know was dementia. Though it is easy to jump to the conclusion that says Martha was a "crazy lady," I couldn't let that be the *only* thing she ever was to me. I had to learn more. How did she end up like that? Though some details about my grandmother remain problematic, her true story (as we now know it) deserves to be fully preserved for future generations and interested historians. This book is our attempt to set the record straight.

What follows is a collective reminiscence built from my own memories, my father Ralph's stories and scrapbooks, my grandfather Louis Jr.'s letters and records, and Martha's own letters and poems. I have also received assistance from wonderfully kind Minnesota historians and genealogy researchers. A special note of gratitude is owed to the following named individuals who added to the collection of family and neighborhood memories which helped us to fully realize Martha's story: Mary Ann Palumbo, Cindy Mitsch, MaryAnn Elias Johnson, Karen Hogendorf, Beth Zabel, and of course, to my daughter, Janelle Molony, who generously produced the book you are now holding.

Illustration 2: Martha Gruening's Lutheran confirmation at St. Paul's Lutheran Church in Henderson, Minnesota, March 27, 1904 (the day after her 14th birthday). She sits in the front row, center-left seat, staring straight into the camera lens.

Credit: Photographer unknown. Courtesy of Ralph Nasch.

Martha's Beginning

Martha Hedwig (nicknamed "Hattie") Gruening, was born March 26, 1890, in Belle Plaine, Minnesota to German immigrants. Not much was written about Martha's mother, Augusta Matilda Seeland, other than a few lines in Martha's poems referring to her as her best pal. Augusta died of bone cancer in 1958. Martha's father, August Ferdinand Gruening was once a soldier in the Prussian army who had taken to a pastoral lifestyle in America on his farmstead near a dairy-creamery. He died from sunstroke in 1903. **(See the Family Trees for further dates and relationships.)**

Little is known about Martha's formative years. In one census record, she reports that she only had a fifth grade education, which may have meant her leaving school to work on the farm at age ten or eleven. She highlights some memories of her farm life in several poems. A brief look into the family's Germanic roots helped us understand some of the challenges my grandmother may have faced while growing up.

In 1881 ship passenger list departing from Hamburg, Germany shows that her parents formerly resided in Köslin, Pommern, a village in the Prussian province of Pomerania (now present-day Koszalin, Poland). After the German-Prussian war of 1866, the German Empire expanded its political boundaries, and by 1871, Prussia was considered a German state (Brandt, E., Bellingham, M., & Cutkomp, K., *Germanic Genealogy*, 2013, 65-66). As historians have explained, "Nineteenth century Germany was a confusing and rapidly changing world, and this ... drove out many Germans who sought a new land where they could establish their homes, farms and families in peace" (Glasrud &

Rankin, "A Heritage Deferred: The German-Americans in Minnesota," 1981, 18).

The immigration record shows the Gruenings sailed to New York before settling in Minnesota. Once in Minnesota, the Gruenings (sometimes spelled "Grüning" in family letters) had six children: Maria ("Mary"), Richard, Hugo ("Hugh"), Martha, Leopold ("Leo"), and Emma. In some descendant's records, the surname which translates to "green" was transformed to "Greening."

Illustration 3: Augusta Gruening (1857 - 1942), Martha's mother. Undated photo. She is featured in several poems as one of Martha's closest friends.

Credit: Possibly taken by Ralph Nasch. Courtesy of Ralph Nasch.

The Anglicized (Americanized) name changes may have been prompted by the onset of World War I and increasing hostilities against Germanic people. According to Minnesota historians, the "German-American assimilation was often coerced

11

and painful" (Glasrud & Rankin, 1981, 18). In historical conference proceedings, experts have explained how Germans in Minnesota were prohibited from speaking their mother tongue in public, many lost their jobs due to employer prejudice, and in some extreme cases, German-Americans were tarred and feathered, or beaten and killed until post-war legislation curbed these behaviors (23).

I never knew any of my grandmother's siblings, though I wish I had met one in particular: Emma, the younger sister that Martha doted on, and who she dedicated her poems to (see illustration 4). My father also said many times that Emma was his favorite aunt over Martha's older sister because Aunt Mary spoke in German and gossiped too much.

My father never met his Uncle Richard, as he died from tuberculosis before Ralph was born. Apparently, Richard wanted to serve in the U.S. military during World War I, but the military wasn't very accepting of Germans at that time. Uncle Hugh liked to hunt and fish, but didn't talk much (*Grandpa Ralph Family History,* 1998). Uncle Leo lived in St. Paul, but had little contact with Ralph. He lost his leg due to tuberculosis and went on to work for an artificial limb manufacturer, before dying in his thirties.

Illustration 4: Emma Augusta Wildemire Gruening (1898 - 1952). Circa 1904-1919. The caption (from Ralph) reads: "My Aunt Emma, mother's sister, and my favorite aunt."

From 1924 to 1930, Emma and her husband, Guy Ellsworth lived one block away from Martha Nasch at 663 Humboldt Avenue.

Credit: Unknown photographer. Courtesy of Ralph Nasch.

Illustration 5: Martha "Hattie" Gruening in her early 20s. Circa 1909.

Credit: Unknown photographer. Courtesy of Ralph Nasch.

When their father, August, died, the loss would have put an immense financial and physical strain on the Gruenings to keep up the farm. Hugh assumed his father's business and took care of their mother.

Eventually, Martha moved to downtown St. Paul and obtained a job at a local hospital, perhaps living with her brother Leo, who resided near Fort Snelling at the time. She made friends with other working girls and enjoyed the spoils of city life by attending the theatre, film houses, symphonies, and dance halls such as the Hiawatha Temple. It was at the Temple, according to her poems, she either met or had a first date with future husband, Louis Nasch Jr., on September 6, 1909.

Illustration 6: Louis Jacob Nasch, Jr. (age 27), 1911.

Credit: Unknown photographer. Courtesy of Ralph Nasch.

Louis Jr.'s Beginning

Louis Jacob Nasch Jr. was born on March 10, 1884 to Louis Jacob

Nasch Sr. and Maria Antonia Doerrler. Louis Jr.'s father came to

St. Paul around 1880 from Haversack, New York. His

grandparents, Mathias Neusch and Elizabeth Grohe (both born in

Alsace, France), immigrated to America in 1846.

My father was taught that the family was and always has

been German, despite the French heritage. It is probable that our

German-speaking Neusch family was Germanic in culture, while French in nationality. Alsace-Lorraine, France is a border region to Germany and boasts intermingled ancestries from both countries. This region was also ceded to the German Empire in 1871 as a result of the Franco-Prussian War. In 1918, after World War I, Alsace-Lorraine was returned to France. Although the Alsasians acculturated with the language and customs, the "new" Germans still considered themselves to be French nationals, regardless of the back-and-forth political boundary changes (Brandt, et. al, *Germanic Genealogy,* 107, 153). For the sake of this introduction, and on my father's insistence, I will continue referring to this family line as German.

Mathias and Elizabeth Neusch had nine children in New York, but only four of them moved to Minnesota, while the rest stayed on the East Coast. Those four (Joseph, Louis Sr., Frank and Rosa) relocated with their parents to the greater St. Paul, Minnesota area in about 1880. The three brothers immediately went into carpentry as laborers, then Louis Sr. eventually opened a deli and grocery at 542-544 Stryker Avenue, in St. Paul's West Side neighborhood. He married Maria Antonia Doerrler in 1882, the same year Mathias died (see illustration 6).

On Louis Jr.'s mother's side, Maria "Antonia" Doerrler was the first child of Valentin Doerrler and Maria Josepha Baumann in Osterburken, Mosbach, Baden (presently Baden-Württemberg,

Germany). Valentin and Maria Doerrler had seven children together, but only three lived past infancy (**see Family Trees**). Then, Valentin died young from injuries he sustained after falling off a roof while fighting a fire in a bucket brigade.

My grandfather has recorded that in the same year his grandmother, Maria, was mourning, her parents pressured her into marrying her second husband, Mr. Sebastian Kahles (from "Bayern," Bavaria, Germany). Like August Gruening, Sebastian Kahles was a Prussian soldier. He went by the nickname "Seefaher," which translates to "sailor." Maria Doerrler bore Sebastian four children who also died in infancy.

In 1874, Sebastian immigrated alone to Philadelphia, Pennsylvania (sometimes referred to as "German town"). Maria initially refused to travel with him, but he convinced her to follow four years later with her surviving children: Maria "Antonia" (22), Joseph Jacob (20), and Katarina "Theresa" (17). Unfortunately, Jacob died from starvation within his first year of arrival after a physician prescribed him a severely restricted diet as a solution to sun stroke. As the story goes, Jacob corresponded with a "quack" doctor in New York by mailing a list of his symptoms and $30.00 USD (the equivalent of $800.00 in 2021), and taking the tragically misguided advice seriously (Nasch, 1958).

In 1880, the (now) family of four relocated to the west side of the Mississippi River, just south of downtown St. Paul, and just west of the "Immigrant Flats" (see Maps). The lowlands immediately west of the Mississippi were nicknamed the "Immigrant Flats" because they flooded whenever the River swelled (Nelson, West Side Flats, St. Paul, 2021). This risk made the former Dakota Indian land inexpensive and accessible to poorer families. Consequently, many European immigrants "flooded" to this city, giving it the moniker. Louis Jr. mentioned the flats in a 1958 letter to Ralph, saying that when his father (Louis Sr.) first came to St. Paul in the Spring of 1880, "The whole west side lower part was under water. All the flats. And way up to where the big steps comes up [sic]." The steps my grandfather referred to were built in 1916 at a staggering eight stories high that functioned, per city historians, as a shortcut through town that connected the "disparate realms of the West Side: below, immigrants, industry, and floods; above, the fabulous views and fine houses of those who prospered" (Nelson, Tour St. Paul, n.d., 6).

Once in St. Paul, Maria Doerrler Kahles started going by "Mary" and she and Sebastian purchased a home on a hill at 642 Hall Avenue, in the "Upper West Side" (above the the flats, see Maps). Their younger daughter, Theresa, purchased the home across the street at house number 637 (Mitsch, C. & Mitsch L.,

2003). Antonia, the eldest daughter, became a cook for Mrs. Grady's fine dining restaurant near 5th and Wabasha streets, downtown.

Illustration 7: Maria Antonia Doerrler (1856 - 1884). Undated painting.

Credit: Painter unknown. Courtesy of Jodi Nasch Decker.

After marrying Louis Nasch Sr., Antonia miscarried one son before Louis Jr. was born in the spring of 1884. She also died tragically, six months later, from medical malpractice. During childbirth, she developed "milk leg," a painful swelling and blood clot in the vein (thrombosis) which was not unheard of, and had a known treatment of applying ice to reduce the inflammation (Nasch, 1958). Her St. Paul physician chose, instead, to lance the leg. We still don't understand what he was trying to accomplish by doing this, but the result was an infection that became life-threatening within six months.

Sensing the urgency, her sister Theresa insisted Louis Sr. consult with a new doctor. So, he brought in Dr. Justus O'Hage, who was a well-known German practitioner in the area. After the examination, Dr. O'Hage told the family, "Too bad for that nice looking woman. If I would of had her three days before this, I would have saved her," (Nasch, 1958).

Louis Nasch Sr., now a widower and a single father, presumably could not care for his infant son while managing the grocery store. He gave over the care of Louis Jr. to his in-laws, the Kahles, who raised Louis Jr. up until the age of seven.

As a child, Louis Jr. helped his grandfather transport beer for local breweries in a two-horse wagon. In the meantime, Louis Sr. married a second time to Amanda Monica Meisinger. Both my father and grandfather used harsh words to express how they felt towards this new woman, though it seemed there was mutual animosity.

When Amanda learned that Louis Jr. was able to work and earn an income, she demanded that he return to his father's home. By then, Louis Jr., had three half-siblings: Henry, Theresa, and Regina. While they attended school, Louis Jr. was put to work for the family in various factories. This was not uncommon prior to compulsory education laws, though he believed the situation was rather unfair. He mentioned working at the "twin hay carpet factory," which might have been the American Grass Twine

Factory at Kent and Doyle streets, though we don't know in what capacity children contributed to the woven rug production (1958). Louis Jr. wrote, "It was a hell of a life," and explained, "It was a mite [mighty] hard thing to leave my grandmother because she was just like my mother" (1958). He never felt loved by Amanda and his childhood tales resonate with classic evil stepmother stories.

After turning eighteen, Louis Jr. promptly moved back into the home of his maternal grandparents (the Kahles) at 642 Hall Avenue. Louis Jr. became a painter and a decorator by trade. A 1930 census shows he worked in a department store, but in Martha's poems, she describes his work as being on a contractual basis as a skilled laborer (see "A Painter" and "Advized By Dad"). My father, Ralph, shared, "A hardship my family had to overcome was living on a low income as my father was out of work many weeks and in those days it was not common or necessary for mothers to work. ... I remember times when he was out of work and we were on relief (welfare). I still recall using food stamps as a child" (*A Grandfather Remembers*, 1987). To make ends meet, Louis Jr. took long-distance jobs. In 1927, he joined a five-month union painting project in Chicago, Illinois. He took an overnight train to come home every two weeks, from April until September (Nasch, 1957).

Per my Louis Jr.'s letters, he recalls meeting Martha through a mutual acquaintance: her brother Leo. Louis Jr. wrote about getting acquainted with Martha at the creamery a few blocks from the Gruening farm" (1957). Leo brought Louis Jr. (then, his good friend) with him on a short visit, where they drank pure buttermilk at the creamery (1957). Leo must have introduced Louis Jr. to his sister at that time.

Illustration 8: Mr. and Mrs. Louis Nasch Jr., September 4, 1913.

Credit: Unknown photographer. Courtesy of Janelle Molony.

Marriage and Children

Four years after their first date, Martha Gruening married Louis Nasch Jr. on September 4, 1913 at the Assumption Catholic Church priest house in St. Paul, Minnesota. Martha was twenty-three and a Lutheran, while Louis was twenty-nine and a Catholic. It was certainly common for young married couples, at the time, to live with the parents of one or the other, until they could become established on their own. Louis Jr. and Martha were no different. Martha joined him in the Kahles home at 642 Hall Avenue. Though Louis Jr.s' grandmother, Mary, passed away in 1911 from senility, both Louis Jr. and Martha took care of Sebastian together until he also passed away of cancer, in 1914.

The St. Paul newlyweds lived in close proximity to other extended family members within their same neighborhood (see Maps). The neighbors factored significantly in Martha and Louis Jr.'s lives. Per the 1930 state census, directly across the street from the Nasches, at 637 and 639 Hall Avenue, lived Louis Jr.'s aunt and uncle, Theresa Doerreler Wiener (Antonia's sister), and Charles Wiener Sr. with Louis Jr.'s cousins, Charles Jr. and his wife, Eva (see illustration 13).

In the next house to the north, number 633, lived another cousin, Anna Rosalia Wiener Paape (Theresa's daughter) and her bartender husband, Arthur Herman Paape (see "An Old Fashion

Dwelling"). For a time, Arthur's brother Friedrich Otto Paape, of Paape's Liquors in South St. Paul, stayed with the Wieners at 637.

Illustration 9: Friends in the yard of 642 Hall Ave., circa 1914-20. (From left to right) Bernard and Clara Frances Wiener Keis (Louis Jr.'s cousins), Martha's sister: Emma Gruening, and Martha and Louis Nasch Jr.

Credit: Unknown photographer. Shared by Debra Kammerer, grand-niece of Clara Keis, via *Ancestry.com*.

Illustration 10: The Wiener family posed in their front yard at 637 Hall Avenue, circa 1904-1914. Charles Sr. is the second from the left, standing. The Nasch home can be seen in the background as the third house from the left. Featured in the middle is the Claus home, and on the left is the Tauring home. One house over to the left (not shown) would be the Hultgren family (**see Maps**).

Immediately to the right is John Volkmeier's home (647 Hall Avenue). John's father, Edward, lived with daughter and son-in-law Esther and John Hultgren, five houses up.

Credit: Unknown photographer. Shared by Cindy Mitsch, great-granddaughter of Charles and Theresa Wiener.

In the last house on this block, 629 Hall Ave., lived first-generation Russian-American Philip Peter Krumm and his new wife, Evelyn. They were close in age with the young Wieners and Paapes. Two of "Pete's" much younger siblings, Carl and Dorothy, who were closer in age to my father, lived around the corner from the Nasches, at 25 Augusta St. W. (present-day Baker St.). My father considered these children as very close playmates (**see illustrations 11 and 35**).

When Martha references a "Mrs. Krumm" in her poem, "Dearest Friend," she could have meant Philip's mother. When some unforeseen trouble presented itself in the Nasch's lives, Martha attributes Mrs. Krumm as being there to help during some of her darkest times.

Illustration 11: June 2, 1929. Ralph (7, right) with Carl Krumm (12) and Dorothy "Doddy" Krumm (10). These neighbors lived diagonally behind the Nasches and they climbed the adjoining fence to play with each other.

Credit: Louis J. Nasch, Courtesy of Janelle Molony.

One house east of Anna Krumm, at 15 Augusta St. W., lived the large Belgian-American Meyers family. One daughter, Agnes Meyers, received a poem from Martha, written to her by request, titled "A Shop Girl."

Finally, between the years of 1924 and 1933, Martha's younger sister, Emma Gruening (then married to Mr. Guy Ellsworth) resided about eight houses away from the Nasches, at 633 Humboldt Ave. (see Maps). To say it was a close-knit community is an understatement, and Martha would come to appreciate the support from her neighbors time and again. They would all play an essential role, specifically helping Martha and Louis Jr. when their first child arrived. It wasn't until after eight years of marriage that my father Ralph was born (November 15, 1921).

Martha was thirty-one when my father was born. As an older mother, she was kept in the West Side Hospital for two weeks after his birth. Louis Jr. brought his newborn home without Martha, and he sought assistance from his female relatives, across the street. Anna Paape's firstborn, Arthur Jr. ("Art," per my father) was born seven months later and they would grow up together as friends and cousins (see illustrations 36 and 37).

Six years later, once again Martha was recovering from a difficult medical procedure and another neighbor lady, Mrs.

Shafer, volunteered to walk Ralph to his first day of school with her own son, George. The Schafer's lived two houses south of the Nasches and George was considered my father's other best friend besides Art (see illustration 26).

Another example of neighbors supporting the family in a time of need was during Martha's confinement at the asylum, Lynette Claus, a teenager from one house to the north, at 636 Hall Ave., supposedly helped Louis Jr. with light housekeeping (see illustration 47). When Martha came home in 1934, Lynette would be an advocate in her defense when her testimony of events came under scrutiny (see Epilogue).

It may have been a challenge to keep one's personal life truly "private," and as I have learned through speaking with descendants from the neighboring families, the airing of one's dirty laundry continues to this day and from their disclosures, we have determined that Martha wasn't the only one with secrets on the street. Some of the gossip, as shared with us, includes the following:

- One descendant's testimony puts Lynette Claus' father, Joe, in the same asylum as Martha, at three different times in his life for crimes related to his excessive drinking and for a bootlegging operation out of the upstairs portion of his home.

- The 1940 census also lists the Nasches' next-door neighbor, Alexander Metzger, at 652 Hall Ave., as a resident of St. Peter's Hospital, for at least four years. He eventually died while in the institution (**see Maps**).

- Across the street, Arthur Paape Sr., was allegedly a drunk and gambler who just "coulden get to quit," in Louis Jr.'s opinion (1958). Curiously, when he died in 1939, Anna married her brother-in-law, "Otto." He was seventeen years her elder and well-off. My grandfather said it was a "smooth move" on her behalf (1958).

- Three houses north of the Nasches, John Hultgren's father, Carl, went "missing" sucpicioulsy after John's mother's died in 1928, per descendant Melodee Beckman's account. Census record searches have helped us locate him in the criminally ill ward of St. Peter's Hospital between 1930 and 1940, before he transferred to a different institution; remaining until his death in 1947 (**see illustration 10 for more about the Hultgren & Volkmeier neighbors**).

Illustration 12: April 15, 1926. "Ralph, 5 years, 5 mo. old."

Martha and son, Ralph, standing in the backyard. Louis Jr. is facing East to take this photograph. One corner of Humboldt High School can be seen in the background, behind the white house.

Credit: Louis Nasch Jr. Courtesy of Ralph Nasch.

Martha's Secret Breakdown

Surprisingly, after scouring everything I could find, and talking to as many living descendants from the neighborhood families as possible, there is still one big mystery that remains unsolved. This is the nature of Martha's mental health decline. Sometime between the first years of their marriage and over the course of the next fifteen years, my grandmother's mental and emotional well-being simmered and brewed, eventually boiling over in 1927. Three reasonable theories explaining how she ended up spending almost seven years in an insane asylum can be narrowed down, based on the family's collective memories and the evidence that remains behind.

One theory involves her conflicting feelings toward motherhood. It is unknown if, in the years leading up to and after Ralph's birth, Martha had difficulty conceiving children, or was ever pregnant with other children. On my father's birth certificate, Martha indicates that he is the only child she had birthed. As early miscarriages might not warrant hospitalization and stillborns did not require a birth or death record yet, family researchers cannot find evidence to indicate any other births.

It is just as easy, however, to speculate that she may have struggled with infertility. If this was the case, she may have endured an untreated physiological or hormonal issue preventing more children. She allegedly told my father that one child was "enough," after explaining that she had a difficult time birthing him (1987).

Illustration 13 (A): Louis Jr.'s caption reads: "Ralph. 5 years, 7 months old. June 15, 1927, after Martha's apraction [sic]." The Weiner home, across the street at 637, can be clearly seen from this point in the Nasches' front yard.

Illustration 13 (B):
(B) Louis Jr.'s caption reads: "June 28, 1927. Right after Martha's apraction [sic]."
Ralph's added caption reads: "She lost weight."

Credits: Louis Nasch Jr. Courtesy of Janelle Molony.

In her poetry, Martha grieves the experience of childbirth and in "Forgotten," she specifically says that after bearing Ralph, she was left weak, helpless and unable to get well. It is at this point, she pinpoints when the devil entered her world (though she points to other moments as well). In another poem, "Cottage," Martha stresses, "When Ralph came in, I was cast out," though this mention appears to be more of a reflection on Louis Jr.'s behavior, as opposed to her own post-partum suffering.

A second theory is related to complications from a surgery that Martha references as the start of all her troubles. Louis Jr. repeatedly documents an operation from June 8, 1927, that left his wife significantly weakened and unable to walk much for many weeks thereafter (**see illustrations 8, 13, 14, 15, and 26**). My grandfather even adds this detail to the back of numerous photographs in the family albums and recorded the event four different times in his epic family reminiscence to Ralph in 1957. Though, Louis Jr. never once mentioned what the surgery was for. Martha never disclosed this information to my father, either. It seems the Nasches agreed to keep this entire operation a secret to their deaths.

Illustration 14:
"Ralph Nasch, July 4, 1927, age 5 years, 7 and ½ months. Martha took picture after her apraction [sic]."

Credit: Martha Nasch. Courtesy of Janelle Molony.

Considering Martha's age in 1927 (thirty-seven), and prior complications with her son's delivery, there are suspicions that her surgery was gynecological in nature. If that were the case, the cultural norm was that a husband would never disclose this information publicly, nor would a mother ever discuss such subjects with a child. If we explore our options (a hysterectomy, a stillbirth, or an abortion), there are significant correlations to her ongoing mental health complaints and weakness. No family records, albums, or correspondence indicate other external issues such as mobility problems, or a serious illness or chronic condition that might necessitate a surgical intervention, or an unbreakable silence.

Illustration 15: Aug. 15, 1926. "Ralph, 4 years, 9 mo. old. Louis took this under the apple tree by the grape vines. Mama is resting her hand up on the grape vine fence. One year later, Martha had her apraction."

Credit: Louis Nasch Jr. Courtesy of Ralph Nasch.

A third theory pointed us to a failing marriage as the antecedent to Martha's mental health breakdown. Martha suggests the moment her world went to hell was when she received evidence of Louis Jr. having an affair (see "Thoughts"). This undoubtedly added to the mental and emotional chaos Martha felt prior to her committal. It is nearly impossible, from what little we know, to pinpoint a date of the alleged affair. Regardless, after finding a perfumed letter in the mail addressed to Louis Jr. from another woman, Martha was filled with bitterness and rancor. She documented her feelings in revenge prose.

In the poem, "Broken Romance," Martha states:

...Once you told me that you loved me and we named our wedding day, then you chose another sweetheart and with me you would not stay.

In another, "Unfaithful," Martha's heartbreak is obvious:

You cried and asked me to forgive and take you back once more. I will forgive and with you live ... With a crushed and broken heart.

Retold in third person, "The Ballad of Martha," she mentions the letter directly:

It was a great surprise. Her heart was crushed and broken, and tears were in her eyes. She said to him we now must part, our wedded life must end.

Although Martha concluded the ballad by calling Louis Jr. a homewrecker, there are always two sides to every story. Surviving family tales (and neighbor accounts) indicate my grandparents had a contentious relationship. In a statement from my father, he said his parents fought in German "when they did not want me to understand" (1998). My father elaborated on this, saying, "My father and mother were not compatible at all, as they had frequent arguments and cussed each other in both English and German ... they argued constantly" (1998).

In addition, there are stories of domestic violence in the home. In another letter, my father reported that "they had frequent arguments with some physical fighting" (1987). Martha's niece, Audry Gruening Rongstad, had once recalled how Martha allegedly threatening her husband with a knife, or actually throwing it at him. Audry also shared that Martha pushed Louis Jr.

off the bed by flipping over the mattress while he was still on it. With no further context to draw from, this hearsay does not account for the possibility of self-defense against anything Louis Jr. may have instigated. It would not be prudent to lean too heavily on any one-sided claim made, especially considering my father's sweeping statements about them both being combative (see "He Said, She Said").

To summarize, a lot of things were not faring well for Martha, and the consequences of the 1927 surgery may have simply been the metaphoric straw that broke the camel's back. Three weeks after the procedure, Martha is noticeably gaunt, her face is drawn, and her expression is more sullen than ever (see illustration 13). Clearly, the surgery had taken a toll on her.

Illustration 16: State Hospital, St. Peter, Minn. Postcard, circa 1908.

Credit: W.S. King. From Library of Congress digital collections.

Was Martha "Hospitalized" or "Sentenced?"

Prior to being committed, Martha sought at least one additional medical consultation with her 1927 doctor-surgeon. She reported to them that since the day of the operation, she had lost her appetite and couldn't eat or drink (**see Epilogue**). It is unknown what remedies were provided to her, if any, other than rest. Clearly, though, after months of no improvement, her doctor was concerned enough to submit to Louis Jr. that Martha required more intensive treatment for her deteriorating condition. However, either through apathy, ignorance, or a lack of medical knowledge, he diagnosed Martha's symptoms as fully mental health-related, rather than considering other physical conditions. Martha disclosed this in a post-asylum interview with the press, saying her reason for hospital admission was "a case of nerves" (**see Epilogue**).

On a frigid January 29, 1928, Martha was brought to the St. Peter State Hospital for the Insane in the city of St. Peter, Minnesota, where she remained for six and one-half years. No medical treatment or diagnostic records have been found on her. We were, however, able to obtain a scanned image of Martha's admission notes from the Minnesota Historical Society (**see illustration 18**). The handwritten record of her entry and exit is simple and sparse, fitting entirely on one 3" x 5" index card. In addition to her name and county of residence, we can see her admission date and patient record number: 20864.

While the precise nature of Martha's diagnosis and treatment are elusive, some reasonable assumptions can be made about her experiences. We've created a general picture of my grandmother's life at St. Peter based on known standard medical and psychiatric treatment practices of the 1920s and 30s, interviews from primary eyewitnesses accounts, through secondary research and by consultations with local historians.

Despite my deepest wish that I could believe all my grandmother's words at face value, I recognize they are coming from a textbook "mental patient," and therefore her credibility may be questioned. In my research, I have used Martha's testimony as a guide, rather than a rule. What I learned, however, was that outside sources do not contradict any of her claims. In fact, they reinforce and validate her story. Several key resources are provided at the end of the Introduction.

The following explores some background on the hospital's development and operations. According to a brochure published by the Minnesota Department of Health Services, the Hospital opened in March, 1866 (2007). At the ten-year point, the hospital, built on hundreds of acres of farmland, could accommodate five hundred patients. By 1906, there were four separate institutions on the property, comprising the mental hospital, a detention hospital, the tuberculosis insane patients, and the criminally insane (2007). The mental hospital was reserved for long-term or custodial patients, whereas the detention hospital was for shorter-term stays. Since 1985, the psychiatric care facility has operated under the new name St. Peter Regional Treatment Center and a historical museum is now situated on the campus.

Dr. Michael Resman's 2013 book, *Asylums, Treatment Centers, and Genetic Jails*, provided an insider look at early hospital operations in Minnesota. Dr. Resman worked at the Rochester State Hospital in Southeastern Minnesota as an occupational therapist. While it's not prudent to conclude that all of the material he includes in his historical research applies to Martha's case, or to St. Peter's Hospital specifically, it certainly suggests industry-wide standards in practice at that time.

Admission to a "lunatic" asylum in the 19th century could stem from a single behavior or emotional state on a long list considered to be antecedents for an eventual case of insanity. Among the reasons Dr. Resman listed were physical injuries, depression, grief, poverty, family desertion, inherited maladies, addictions, hysteria, and senility (*Asylums*, 2013, 14). Simply being observed or suspected of these behaviors was enough to generate a psychiatric referral. Other catch-all reasons people could be committed were: domestic troubles, a disappointed affection, menstrual irregularities, religious excitement, nymphomania, and general moodiness. The criteria seemed like a mixed bag of medical care, penitentiary reform, moral reform, physician experimentation, and the more well-known safehouse "Asylum" for the most extreme mental health cases.

Based on first-person accounts researched by Dr. Phyllis Chesler, author of the 1972 book *Women and Madness,* arriving at the hospital could have included an arrest by a sheriff, either at the local home, or by being picked up from wherever one was out and about for the day (as cited in Geller & Maxine's *Women of the Asylum,* 1994, xx). A male next of kin might use the excuse of going somewhere non-alarming to get their female relative into a vehicle, Dr. Chesler explained, then he'd escort her to meet with "a judge and/or physician, who certified her 'insane' on her husband's say-so" (Geller & Maxine, xx). With the relative's accusation and physician's agreement, the judge would provide an initial sentencing for psychiatric holding until the receiving hospital's psychiatrist could update the treatment plan with further assessments.

Upon admission, Martha would have been processed through the intake experience, just as any other patient of the time. New patients were given an initial bath and a one-style-fits-all bowl haircut (possibly for sanitary reasons, as lice and mites were common and highly transmissible). Beth Zabel, a volunteer coordinator and asylum museum docent explained that on entry, female patients were issued a denim sack dress with socks, but extra underwear was not always available for them (personal communication to Jodi Nasch Decker, 2021). There are no known photos of Martha during her stay at the hospital to illustrate any of this.

Illustration 17: July 4, 1927. "Ralph, 5 years old."

Ralph wrote about the time when his mother was in the State Hospital, "My father raised me during this period and I recall being very lonely when alone at home. I could go to neighbors for help, but there were no 'sitters' for me. Fortunately, we had a large yard and the neighbor kids all congregated there frequently" (*A Grandfather Remembers*, 1987).

Credit: Martha Nasch. Courtesy of Janelle Molony.

Meals at the hospital consisted mainly of boiled vegetables in broth, eaten in metal bowls (Resman, 108). Some patients were given extra servings of butter and milk to maintain their body weight (Zabel, 2021). Cleansing baths (as opposed to hydrotherapy baths) were only offered once or twice a week, and patients used group lavatories with "no privacy ... no toilet paper or even toilet seats" (Resman, 108).

Another highly informative source comes from news journalist Geri Hoffner who produced "Minnesota Bedlam," a six-article series of investigative reports about Minnesota's mental health facilities (1948, *Minneapolis Morning Tribune*). This exposé came out on the heels of the shocking 1946 *Time* magazine feature piece, "Bedlam," about state-run mental health facilities in Pennsylvania and Ohio. Per Geri's observations of St. Peter's, patient conditions had not shown substantial improvement even ten years after Martha's departure. From what she saw, she reported that patients had assigned beds, but rarely had sheets or pillowcases (Hoffner, *Minneapolis Morning Tribune,* 1948, May 13).

Dr. Resman had said just as much in his book, but explained that due to overcrowding, some hospitals were forced to fill dormitories with back-to-back rows of beds in rows "with barely enough room to squeeze between," and temporarily line the hallways … with fold-away beds (Resman, *Asylums*, 2013, 108). Private rooms were not generally available to the middle or lower classes, as Martha was.

When Louis Jr. and Ralph visited Martha, Ralph did not recall seeing such bleak conditions, nor does he recall her having roommates or other patients ever being around. I have since confirmed that the hospital used nicely furnished rooms for visitations, rather than actual patient wards.

Another patient, made anonymous with the pseudonym Jim Curran, who was hospitalized at St. Peter's for a portion of the time as Martha, has stated in his memoir, that "receiving visitors was, of course, our most exciting contact with the outside world" (Krauch, *A Mind Restored*, 1937, 119). He described the visiting room as a sunny room with bright colors, nice oak furniture, and vases of flowers. Visitors never saw the living conditions of quiet patients on the second floor, nor would they hear the constantly screaming patients on the third floor, per Elsa Krauch's retelling of Jim's experience.

Patients such as Martha, may have received treatment as detailed in *The St. Peter State Hospital Museum* book, published in 2016 by the St. Peter State Hospital Museum Committee. Procedures and treatments being administered in the 1930's included, "insulin and metrazol shock therapies, electro-convulsive shock therapy, [and] prefrontal lobotomy surgery" (St. Peter, 5).

Other treatments utilized at this time were hydrotherapy (which was the prolonged use of baths), electrotherapy "baths" (prolonged exposures to static electricity) and the combination of both water and electricity in which electrodes are either submerged in a patient's bathwater, or otherwise attached to the tub.

In the six and one-half years my grandmother lived at St. Peter, she probably experienced some of these treatments at one time or another, although we can not independently verify that. The Museum Committee reported, unfortunately, that between the years of 1890 and 1954, "there was no effective treatment during these years for serious mental illness" (St. Peter, 16).

Over time, the state hospitals underwent reforms in terms of patient treatments, and their operating protocols became more progressive. One historian at the hospital reported that there were therapeutic programs and activities available for patients such as dance classes, sewing groups, a small farm, and a functional garden. Dr. Resman stated that female patients were particularly encouraged to practice their embroidery, tatting, and help with knitting stockings (*Asylums,* 2013, 15). In some of the sister institutions, patients participated in choral music and plays, watched weekly movies, had access to a library and even to a beauty parlor. Dr. Resman further reported, depending on one's interests, patients could participate in a sports team, unless their health was problematic, or if they were considered a flight risk (111).

Photos and narratives released from the Minnesota Historical Society and the St. Peter State Hospital Museum have shown that patients decorated for and celebrated the holidays with dances and themed activities. Former patient, Jim Curran, said about the festivities he attended, "the thought of a dance in a mental hospital filled me with horror," but once the music began, he said it was a delightful affair (Krauch, 75-76).

Regardless of how humane the conditions eventually became, my grandmother did not perceive her experience to be so. If we look at Martha's poem, "The Asylum," she paints a distinctly different picture from what some of the museum docents and brochures describe. She wrote:

> *This place is like a factory, they come in day by day. Some of them restored to health ... Some are so violent they rave and rant. ... Some are a total wreck ... They do not know they are alive, have not a word to say.*

About those Martha may have "socialized" with at the pleasant gatherings, she stated:

We sit in here so lonely, our eyes are blurred and wet... for days, for months, and years, just waiting, waiting for our death.

When reporter Geri Hoffner visited the Minnesota hospitals, living conditions sounded similar to Martha's depiction: people sleeping on cots in hallways and corridors, and hundreds of patients who"sit their lives away ... dejected, hopeless," some wearing belts, ankle cuffs or "mittens" (a gentler name for shackles) which keep them strapped in place due to a lack of available attendants (*Minneapolis Morning Tribune*, May 13, 1948). On meals, she found that the per-meal budget for patients was the equivalent of $.90 cents, USD in 2021, and food was often tasteless and served cold, and without butter, as other historians have suggested (May 18).

Based on a 1930 census of the institution, Martha did not have an assigned chore or job, nor are any mentioned in her writing. Hoffner's investigation revealed that patients were never forced to participate in such activities, but if they choose not to, their only other option was to remain seated on a hard bench doing nothing, in perpetuity (*Minneapolis Morning Tribune*, 1948, May 14). Another eyewitness account, this time from former patient H.H. Hanley, as reported to Alice Russell (another former patient who investigated hospital conditions after her own release) states that "patients were compelled to do drudgery which was the duty of the attendants, being told they must do it if they wanted to get out" (as cited in *Women of the Asylum*, 1994, 198).

Historian Beth Zabel has since countered these comment with an assurance that because work was considered therapeutic, "all patients who could work were encouraged to do so" (personal communication to Janelle Molony, October 22, 2021). Since patients were needed to help run the farm, wash the laundry, cook, and clean (due to inadequate staffing, as Hoffner found), it's reasonable to assume Martha would have helped with something. After all, she reported she was cognizant enough, being "normal in every other way," as quoted in a post-release newspaper interview (**see Epilogue, illustration 46**).

In that same interview, Martha disclosed to a reporter that while at the asylum, she hid or threw away her food, and that hospital staff tried to force-feed her. Dr. Resman verified in his book that, as needed, "patients who refused to eat were force-fed," noting that this policy produced better results than the previous practice of waiting for a patient to eat on their own (*Asylums*, 2013, 32). He stated without irony that the former method "resulted in most of them dying" (32).

When I read through eyewitness testimonies of force-feeding, I was shocked by reports of broken teeth, spoons tearing at the soft palate, burns by hot liquids, choking on bites of food that were too large to swallow, and even death. Joining this list of horrors, Martha's scathing eyewitness account of a patient being force-fed spares no gruesome detail in her poem, "Mary."

Borrowing a quote from Ruth Hahn, author of the 1984 book, *Oh, You work at the Bughouse!*, Dr. Resman shared another graphic description of patients being intubated for feedings: patients "gagged and squirmed all over the bed while the doctor tried to inch the tube down" (*Asylums*, 120).

Attempts to reduce the physical trauma of force-feeding began nearly forty years before my grandmother's residency. Turn of the century reformist, Dr. William A. Hammond, author of *The Non-Asylum Treatment of the Insane*, wrote in his research findings that some patients may have erroneously believed that their food was poisoned, or may have intentionally tried to commit suicide via starvation, which required staff intervention (1880). On being force-fed, he explained that "the operation ... is a delicate one, requiring anatomical skill; and yet it is one which in American asylums is often left to be performed by ignorant and brutal attendants, a physician not even being present" (Hammond, 1880). He recommended that folks who refuse food, are potentially suicidal, or who have delusions about food, should be "sequestrated" (isolated or hidden away), for this particular procedure (Hammond, 1879).

When I looked for examples of such patients with food-refusing behaviors, former patient H.H. Hanley provided concerns from when she was assigned work in the kitchen. She learned patients were liable to have their food drugged at any time at the will of their physicians or attendants" (as disclosed to another patient, Alice Russell in *Women of the Asylum*, 1994, 198). From this, we can see that, sometimes, what Dr. Hammond called an "erroneous" belief and "delusional," was not so, at least at the "brutal" American asylum of St. Peter, Minnesota.

Other accounts have assured us of a gentler approach to handling food-avoidance, such as that observed by Dr. William Erickson, who was once a medical director of the hospital. He stated in his 1991 book, both "ether and chloroform were occasionally used to quiet violent patients, or to anesthetize patients who would not eat for delusional reasons," (*The Great Charity*, 31). Once in a twilight sleep, patients would be intubated and fed a liquid meal. If, in the process, patients weakened past a certain point of responsiveness, hospital workers would administer a tonic called spiritus frumenti (iron in a wine base) that would "stimulate the appetite and revive weakened patients" (31).

Though I don't personally believe my grandmother was delusional, in the historical research text, *Investigating the Body in*

50

the Victorian Asylum, Dr. Jennifer Wallis detailed that it was the common belief of psychiatric doctors at the turn of the century, that sensory distortions were the effect of delusional thinking, and treated as such (2017, 43).

While I am not privy to Martha's prognosis or prescribed treatment plan, documentation showed she left the property before her official discharge date. Remarks written on her admission record, under the column "escaped," include two date entries. The first says August 29, 1930, then a second entry is for June 26, 1934 (**see illustration 18**). On both occasions, she was marked as returned the next day. Her second escape was only three weeks before her parole, which may indicate she was unaware of a plan for an early release, or simply didn't want to wait one day longer.

Beth Zabel has clarified that not all patients "escaped" in a "runaway" sense. Rather, milder patients could roam freely on and off the hospital's campus with permission. Some even held part-time jobs in the nearby city, such as babysitting and housekeeping (for women), and day labor or seasonal farm work (for men) (personal communication to Janelle Molony, 2021).

There's no evidence that Martha was ever granted the level of patient freedom that would allow her to roam on her own. It is also unknown what disciplinary action may have resulted to curb unauthorized departures. Where Martha went, how far, and the precipitating motives for her escapes are still mysteries that will remain locked away forever. If she was wearing a hospital gown, though, she would have been easy to spot in the nearby town or countryside.

When discussing these findings with my father, he said he had no knowledge of these "great escapes" and could not provide additional commentary on them. Martha did, however, write one poem that uncharacteristically takes readers on a wild journey with an escaped criminal on a bucking bronco (**see "The Fated Chase"**).

NAME	Nasch,Martha L.		NO.	20864

COUNTY   Ramsey

ADMITTED TO   St. Peter Hosp--------Jan. 27,1928

INSTITUTION NO. *18115*

TRANSFERRED TO

DISCHARGED *Aug. 19, 1935* ✓

READMITTED   DISCHARGED

DIED

RELEASED FROM PAYMENT BY BOARD   3-26-28

REMARKS

TRANSFERRED TO FILE "B"

PAROLED	RETURNED
July 29, 1934 ✓	

ESCAPED	RETURNED
Aug. 29, 1930	*Aug. 30, 1930*
June 26, 1934 ✓	*June 27, 1934*

Illustration 18: "Martha L. Nasch" Hospital admission ticket.

Credit: Courtesy of Minnesota Historical Society.

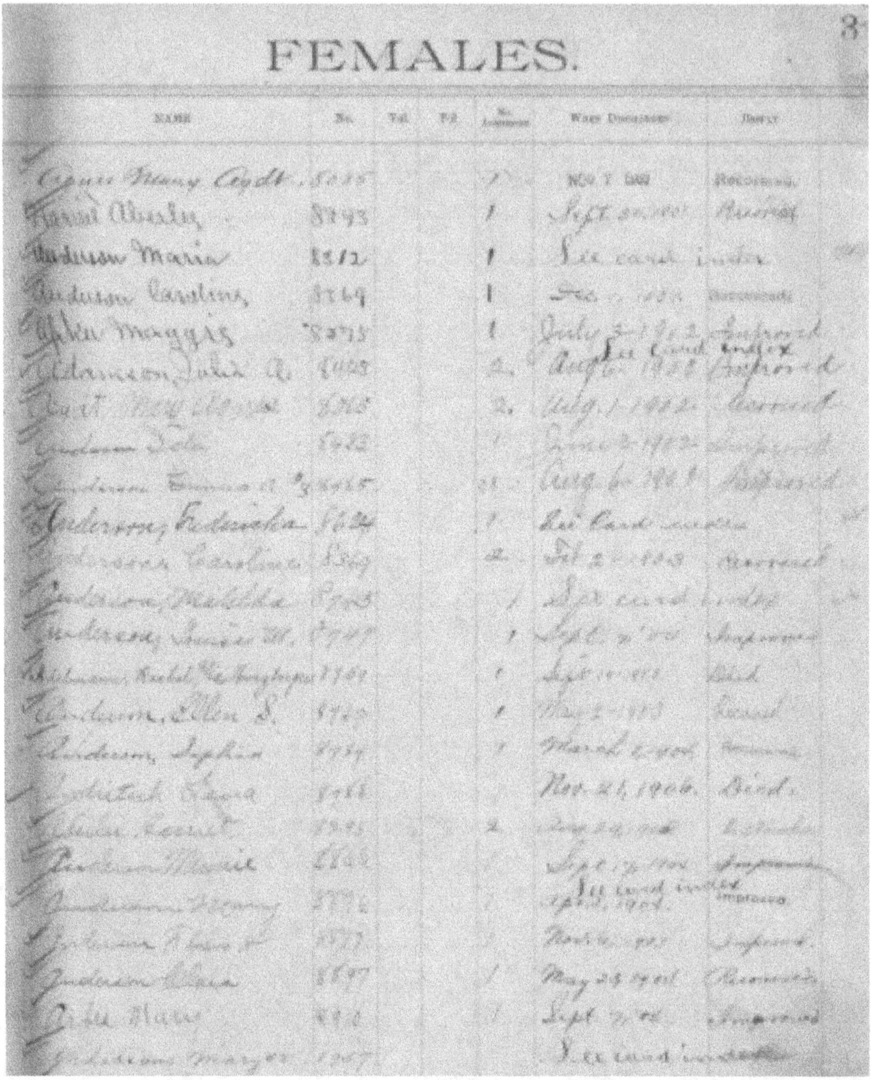

Illustration 19: Example page from a 1904 patient casebook. Martha's casebook entry (not shown) reads: "Nasch, Martha L. Residence: St. Paul, Minn. Admitted: Jan. 27, 1928. Discharged: Aug. 19, 1935. Remarks: Improved" (per the Minnesota Historical Society's transcription).

Credit: Minnesota Division of Public Institutions, Patient Registers and Indexes, 1864-1924.

Did She Ever Recover?

Martha eventually presented herself as sufficiently recovered and left the asylum in 1934. We know, based on her later testimony, that she spent time during and after her committal researching her condition by reading scientific books made available in the hospital's library and by searching within Biblical scripture.

On September 18, 1934, she told a news reporter: "I found a plausible explanation in the Bible ... Although I never had paid much attention to the Bible up to that time" (**see Epilogue, illustration 46**). She then quoted an Old Testament Bible scripture from 2 Kings 7:2: "They shall see food, but not eat. It shall be of wormwood. They shall see water, but not drink." She also mentions wormwood as a poison in the poem, "Suffering." Martha then affirmed, "That describes perfectly my condition, but I cannot understand why this curse should be visited on me."

While her spiritual beliefs should not be too quickly dismissed as a way mental illnesses can manifest, her statements about being cursed, or perhaps being afflicted by a demon, would fall far outside the treatment scope of conventional psychiatry. For a spiritual problem, then, she sought a spiritual answer.

One possibility for her regaining enough sanity to settle her "case of nerves" comes from Martha being persuaded by Christian Science philosophies. One that may have influenced her is that human bodies were designed to enjoy food and drink, but not be overly dependent upon them (pointing to how only a higher power can sustain one's life). The concept of fasting (or reducing food intake) is thousands of years old. The faster must increase their level of dependence on a higher power, and as a result of this spiritual refinement or detox from the gluttony of eating more than necessary, one could benefit from radical healing that is activated when bodies are in a state of ketosis.

A modern practice coined "Breatharianism" was popularized in the 1950s, through the writings of dietitian Hilton Hotema (the pen name of author George Clements). He kept to a fruitarian or juice-only diet and proclaimed it to be a miraculous answer to many of life's deadly conditions. Hotema referenced my grandmother's nutritional abstinence as a remarkable example of a spiritual achievement in both his texts, *Man's Higher Consciousness* (1962, pp. 9, 43) and *Empyreal Sea* (1964, p. 16). Hotema's mention of Martha has since elevated his reader's perception that she was a high-level Breatharian. The claim is near to impossible, considering the Breatharian practice was not widely recognized during Martha's search for answers. In addition,she declared that not eating was a "curse" on her, as opposed to a personal choice, as Breatharians have (**see Epilogue, illustration 48**). It is difficult for me to believe my grandmother would ever have consented to representing the Breatharians at large, especially because of how she was treated in the first place for her complaints.

Whether by spiritual or medical means, Martha met some sort of criteria to be released on July 29, 1934. Dr. Resman provided clarity on the patient release protocols, saying, "a committed insane person didn't have to prove they had recovered" (41). Hospital historian Beth Zabel added, "despite her delusions, if [Martha] was otherwise healthy, she could be discharged" (communication to Jodi Nasch Decker, 2021). This might explain why Martha continued saying she never ate, even when she returned home. For Martha, it would be her (alleged) cheating husband who would have to welcome her home. She had no other legal options at that time. It was well-known that "a male family member would [have] to take responsibility," says Zabel, as a way to ensure a patient's chances for remaining stable after their treatment (2021).

In my opinion, was Martha ever "cured?" It's hard to say, but her patient record did include the discharged notation: "Improved" (Minnesota Historical Society, see illustration 19). Her official discharge date reads August 19, 1935. From her early parole date until then, we can comfortably assume she received medical check-ups or other community supervision. From Dr. Jeffrey Gellar and Dr. Maxine Harris's studies on early Twentieth Century

Illustration 20: Martha stands with her sister, Mary, in her front yard, two years after her release.

The caption reads: "Last of June, 1936. Mary & Martha at our homestead."

Credit: Louis Nasch Jr. Courtesy of Janelle Molony.

hospital standards, we know that "social workers were assigned to coordinate discharge planning and provide environmental care for patients who were newly discharged" (*Women of the Asylum,* 1994, 185). Because patients at St. Peter's were most certainly medicated, (specifically with sedatives such as Laudanum and Sodium Barbital, per Dr. Resman), it's possible, as a condition of her release, Martha may have required medication management until she'd tapered off. Social workers may have also checked-in with the patient's social contacts about their progress and behaviors, post-release (Geller & Harris, 185).

Unfortunately, there was no happy ending for Martha and Louis Jr. AFter six years home, and just as soon as Ralph turned eighteen, the Nasches divorced. My father had said that Martha never forgave Louis Jr. for her being committed.

After the divorce, Martha took a job and moved to the Highland Park neighborhood, in the southwest corner of St. Paul. The years of separation from her son, no doubt, took a toll on their relationship.

My father chose to remain living with Louis Jr., who had been the mainstay of his childhood years, described as doting and hardworking. He remarked, "[My dad] would do a lot for me and give me the shirt off his back" (Nasch, 1987).

Illustration 21:
"Mother's Day. Ma. 52, Pa, 57," 1941.

The Nasches were divorced on November 6, 1941 with the assistance of Louis Jr.'s cousin and lawyer, Ed. Meissinger (his stepmother's nephew).

Louis Jr. called the divorce a "God blessing for the both of us and for your sake, Ralph."

Credit: Photographer unknown. Courtesy of Janelle Molony.

Illustration 22: September 1, 1945. Martha Nasch (55) married William "Bill" Lehman (64).

According to Ralph, "Bill was a good stepfather and I had a friendly relationship with him" (*A Grandfather Remembers*, 1987). Both moved into the Good Samaritan nursing home near Gaylord, Minnesota, and lived out their final days: Martha passing away in 1970 and William in 1975.

Credit: Unknown photographer. Courtesy of Ralph Nasch.

Martha returned to dating after Louis Jr., and suspected she was cheated on by others, based on a disclosure made in a 1945 letter to my mother, Marie Nasch. Then, in September 1945, Martha married Mr. William "Bill" Lehman (1891-1975) from Sibley County, near where Martha grew up. My father believed she was happy with Bill (who was also on his second marriage). There was no further indication by any family members that Martha ever experienced the same relationship difficulties with Bill as she'd had with Louis Jr.

From 1965 to 1970, Martha declined in health, struggling with diabetes and then dying from a heart attack or stroke, per her death certificate. By then, whatever truly prompted Martha's breakdown went with her to the grave. By then, all remaining secrets surrounding her asylum committal went with her to the grave. Louis Jr. also took his secrets to the grave on October 13, 1964. As my father tells the story, my grandfather dropped dead from a heart attack while mowing the yard he'd maintained with pride (as featured in many of Martha's poems). A neighbor discovered his body in the yard and notified Ralph (see illustration 35 to learn who).

After the completion of my research, I am left with a great deal of compassion towards my grandmother for what she endured in the 1920s and 30s. While many of her story details were disturbing for me to consider and uncomfortable to address, through this historical exploration, I have gained a better appreciation for how formidable of a woman she must have been to persevere through nearly seven years of involuntarily experimental treatments that we would now label as traumatizing. Still, I have a sense that she wouldn't tolerate being pitied over it, and I, too, have chosen to see her as resilient and as a survivor.

Chapter References

Beckman, M. (2021, October 15). [Personal Communication to Janelle Molony] Austin, Minnesota.

Brandt, E. R., Bellingham, M., Cutkomp, K., Frye, K., Lowe, P. A., & Sternberg, P. (2013). *Germanic genealogy: A guide to worldwide sources and migration patterns.* St. Paul, MN: Germanic Genealogy Society.

Erickson, W. (1991). *This Great Charity.* St. Peter, MN: St. Peter Regional Treatment Center.

Geller, J., Harris, M. (1994). *Women of the Asylum: voices from Behind the Walls, 1840-1945.* New York, NY: Anchor Books.

Hoffner, G. (1948, May 13). Minnesota Bedlam: Mentally Ill Need Care... *Minneapolis Morning Tribune.*

Hoffner, G. (1948, May 14). Minnesota Bedlam: Mental Patients Sit... *Minneapolis Morning Tribune.*

Hoffner, G. (1948, May 15). Minnesota Bedlam: Attendants Hoe Hard Row. *Minneapolis Morning Tribune.*

Hoffner, G. (1948, May 17). Minnesota Bedlam: Mentally Ill Get Little Help. *Minneapolis Morning Tribune.*

Hoffner, G. (1948, May 18). Minnesota Bedlam: Patients Fed 8-Cent Meals. *Minneapolis Morning Tribune.*

Hoffner, G. (1948, May 13). Minnesota Bedlam: Chains Don't Cure Minds. *Minneapolis Morning Tribune.*

Hotema, H. (1962). *Man's Higher Consciousness.* Pomeroy, WA: Health Research.

Hotema, H. (1964). *Empyreal Sea.* Pomeroy, WA: Health Research.

Krauch, E. (1937). *A Mind Restored: The Story of Jim Curran.* New York, NY: G.P. Putnam's Sons

Minnesota Department of Human Services (2007, October). *The Evolution of State Operated Services* [Brochure]. St. Paul, MN: Minnesota Department of Human Services.

Mitsch, C. & Mitsch, L. (2003). "Charles Wiener and Theresa Doerrler," Keis Family History Papers. Unpublished Manuscript.

Nasch, L. J. (1957, March 6). Louis J. Nasch Jr. Reminiscence [Letter to Ralph Nasch]. St. Paul, Minnesota.

Nasch, L. J. (1958, February 27). [Letter to Ralph and Marie Nasch]. St. Paul, Minnesota.

Nasch, L. J. (1963, July 29). [Letter to Ralph and Marie Nasch]. St. Paul, Minnesota.

Nasch, M. H. (1932). [Book of Poems]. St. Peter, Minnesota.

Nasch, M. H. (1945, March 23). [Letter to Marie Nasch]. St. Paul, Minnesota.

Nasch, L. J. (1958, February 27). [Letter to Ralph and Marie Nasch]. St. Paul, Minnesota.

Nasch, R. L. (1987, August 20). A Grandfather Remembers [Reminiscence]. Tempe, Arizona.

Nasch, R. L. (1998, January). [Letter to Johanna Marie Nasch].Tempe, Arizona.

Nelson, P. (n.d.). Tour St. Paul [Interpretive Guide], *Historic St. Paul.* Accessed August 31, 2021 from https://www.historicsaintpaul.org/tour-west-side

Nelson, P. (2021, May 15). West Side Flats, St. Paul, Minnesota, *Minnesota Historical Society.* Accessed June 22, 2021 from http://www.mnopedia.org/place/west-side-flats-st-paul

Resman, M. (2013). *Asylums, Treatment Centers, and Genetic Jails: A History of Minnesota's State Hospitals.* St. Cloud, MN: North Star Press.

St. Peter Hospital Hospital Museum Committee. (2016). *The St. Peter State Hospital Museum.* St. Peter, Minnesota

Hammond, W. A. (1879). *The Non-Asylum Treatment of the Insane.* New York, NY: G.P Putnam's Sons.

Hammond, W. A. (1880). The Treatment of the Insane. *The International Review*, VII(March), pp. 225-241.

Wallis, J. (2017). *Investigating the Body in the Victorian Asylum.* Cham, Switzerland: Palgrave MacMillan.

Zabel, B. (2021, May 19). [Personal Communication to Jodi Decker] St. Peter, Minnesota.

Zabel, B. (2021, October 22). [Personal Communication to Janelle Molony] St. Peter, Minnesota.

Family Trees &

Neighborhood Maps

Gruening Line, Immigrated to U.S.A. in 1881

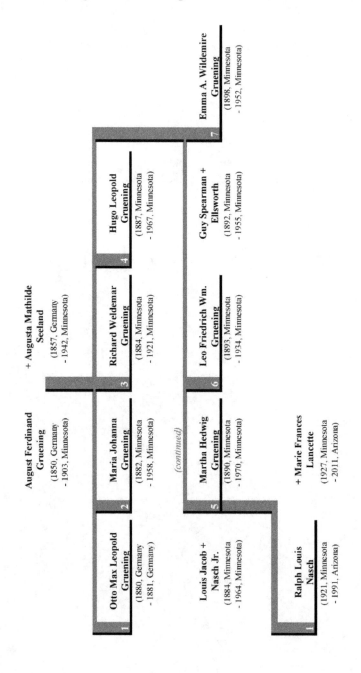

Nasch Line, Immigrated to U.S.A. in 1846

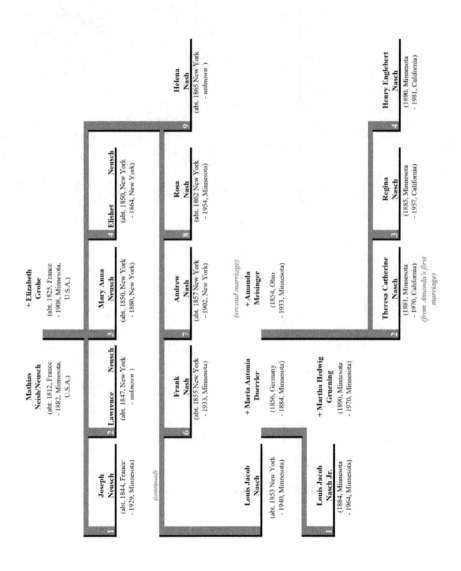

Mathias Neish/Neusch
(abt. 1812, France
- 1882, Minnesota,
U.S.A.)

+ Elizabeth Grohe
(abt. 1825, France
- 1908, Minnesota,
U.S.A.)

Joseph Neusch
(1844, France
- 1929, Minnesota)

Lawrence Neusch
(abt. 1847, New York
- *unknown*)

Mary Anna Neusch
(abt. 1850, New York
- 1880, New York)

Elisbet Neusch
(abt. 1850, New York
- 1864, New York)

Helena Nash
(abt. 1865 New York
- *unknown*)

Frank Nash
(abt. 1855 New York
- 1933, Minnesota)

Andrew Nash
(abt. 1857 New York
- 1902, New York)

Rosa Nash
(abt. 1862 New York
- 1954, Minnesota)

(continued)

Louis Jacob Nash
(abt. 1853 New York
- 1940, Minnesota)

+ Maria Antonia Doerrler
(1856, Germany
- 1884, Minnesota)

+ Martha Hedwig Gruening
(1890, Minnesota
- 1970, Minnesota)

(second marriage)

+ Amanda Meisinger
(1854, Ohio
- 1933, Minnesota)

Louis Jacob Nasch Jr.
(1884, Minnesota
- 1964, Minnesota)

Theresa Catherine Nasch
(1881, Minnesota
- 1970, California)
(from Amanda's first marriage)

Regina Nasch
(1885, Minnesota
- 1957, California)

Henry Englebert Nasch
(1890, Minnesota
- 1981, California)

Doerrler Line, Immigrated to U.S.A. in 1874-78

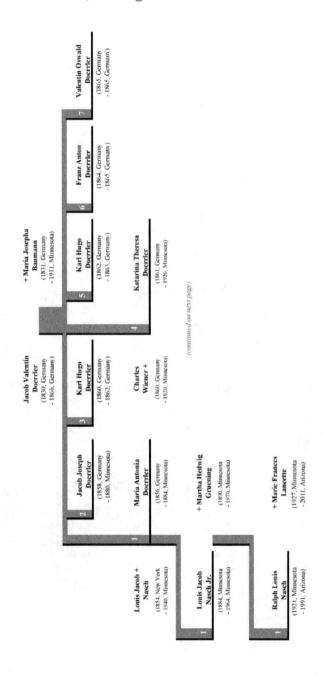

(continued on next page)

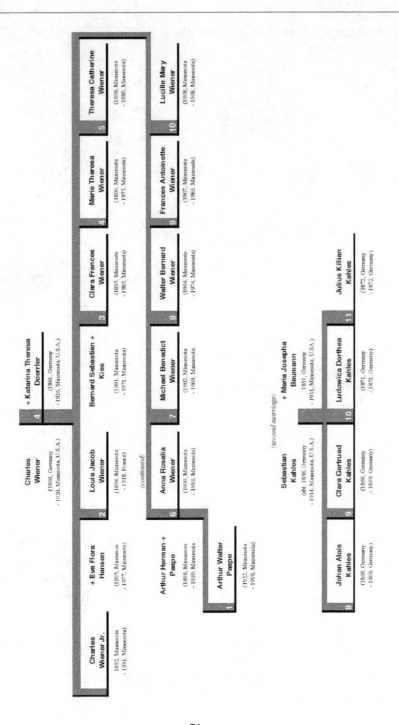

St. Paul, Minnesota: West Side Neighborhood Maps

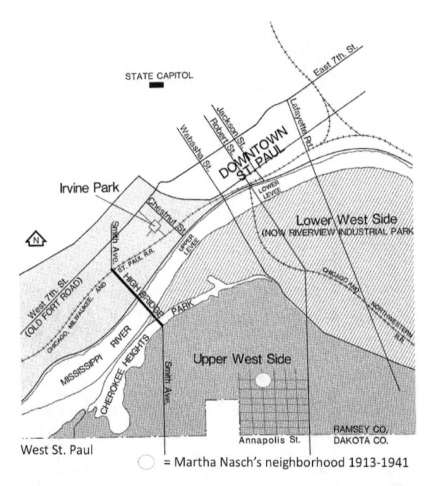

= Martha Nasch's neighborhood 1913-1941

Map 1: 1985 map of St. Paul, Minnesota's "West Side," showing the Minnesota River and "Immigrant Flats." Martha Nasch's neighborhood near Hall Ave. and present-day Baker St. is marked with a white circle, just a few blocks from the city of West St. Paul.

Credit: Original map by Steve Anderson (MN/DOT), as published in the MN Department of Transportation's photo essay, *St. Paul's High Bridge: 1889-1985*. Nasch neighborhood details were added by Janelle Molony.

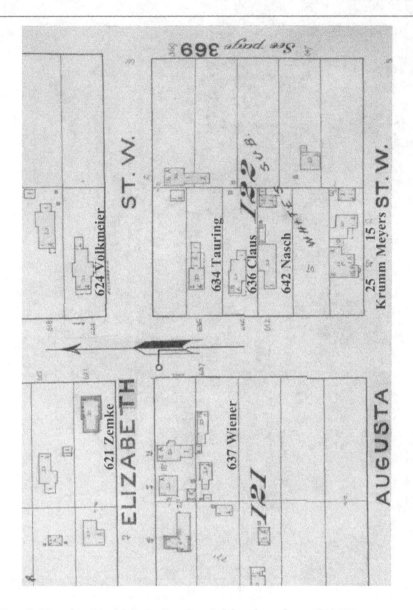

Map 2: Martha Nasch's St. Paul neighborhood as of 1905.

Credit: Created using 1905 census data and a modified plat map in *Atlas of St. Paul, Minnesota, 1891,* from the University of Minnesota (Digital Library).

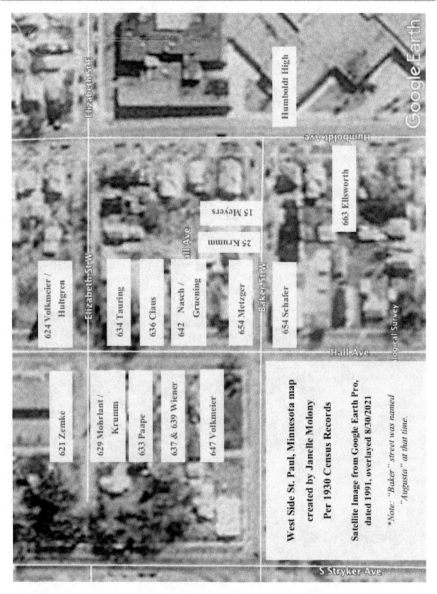

Map 3: Martha Nasch's St. Paul neighborhood as of 1930.

Credit: Created using data from a 1930 U.S. State Census record and a 1991 satellite image from Google Earth Pro.

Map 4: Street views of 642 Hall Avenue. In "A Castle," Martha details the house as painted green. The large, front yard tree may be the grim focal point of focus in "A Cottonwood Tree." Several other poems describe the property, including "A Painter" and "Home."

Credit: (Left) 1954 photograph by Louis J. Nasch. Courtesy of Ralph Nasch. (Right) 2021 screenshot from Google Earth satellite view.

Poems Dated 1928-1932

I: What Makes Me Mad?

Illustration 23: Martha with Louis J. Nasch Jr., circa 1911. Presumed to be an engagement photo.

Credit: Geo. F. Coan, at 499 Wabasha St.St. Paul, Minn. Courtesy of Ralph Nasch.

1. "Thoughts"

I picture a scene of which I once knew.

Before I was forsaken by almighty power...

The devil attacked.

He led me off track

And yearned for my soul to devour.

To one, it all seems but a dream

That two hearts were joined into one...

Our romance was shattered,

Our futures were battered

And faded away, like the sun.

I'm millions of miles from nowhere.

I have no world, nor a home...

To those I one time knew

On Earth, wide and blue,

I'll send them my thoughts in a poem.

2. "The Ballad of Martha"

A sweet and pretty maiden, who lived in a country home,
Sought futures and adventures, so she decided to roam.
She went to explore the big city and scenes so large, to view.
There were attractions everywhere, of which she never knew.
Her old country life was peaceful. How different life now seemed.
And, while away from mother, of back home she'd oft-times dreamed.

She soon became acquainted with bustling city life,
And sought out more of its pleasures, without knowing of strife.
She went to shows and dramas, the ballroom was her delight.
There, she met a handsome fellow who walked her home at night.
She liked his way of wooing. He was so gentle and sweet.
He took her to a tea room and bought her nice things to eat.

After four years of courtship they had spent in happy life,
They chose to be united into one man and his wife.
Their home, at first, seemed happy. It was free from woe and care.
But it wasn't how it should have been to have babies there.
Many idle hours she had. To more dances she would go,
While hubby took another course, of which she did not know.

[cont.]

One day, there came a letter. It contained a great surprise.

Her heart was swift crushed and broken, and tears poured from her eyes.

She said to him, "We now must part. Our wedded life must end."

"I've a letter addressed to you. It's from your lady friend."

Their home was wrecked. Their hearts were sad.

Each went their different way.

He said that he would not admit that he had gone astray.

He followed his wife all over to win her back again.

She said her heart had turned to stone, that she was thru with men.

After months of struggles, to her seemed more like a year,

She went back to her mother's home for comfort and for cheer.

How sadly romance ended for she, the faithful wife,

Who would have chose to die for him, if ever to save his life.

Editorial Comments

Originally titled: "Fate."
The "futures and adventures" idea is reprised in #61 "Futures and Advantures."

The ballroom where Martha danced with Louis is identified in another poem as the Hiawatha Temple, located near 5th and Wabasha streets in downtown St. Paul.

The tea reference may be the Tea Room at the Emporium, a high-end multistory department store located at the corner of Minnesota and Robert streets, just across from the Golden Rule (another department store).

The letter Martha mentioned here is likely one and the same as referenced in the poem, "Perfumed Kindness."

The timing of this alleged affair is up for discussion. On one hand, if the event happened after Ralph was born, it would have been highly controversial (nearly unspeakable) for a mother to walk out on her husband when a child was involved in the story, short of tremendous abuse or other endangerment. On the other hand, the focus on this theme in her journal suggests the event occurred near enough to Martha's committal to keep her seething.

The comment, "We must now part," shows Martha may have tried to initiate either a divorce or formal separation, though obtaining either, at that time, required fault to be assigned. Martha would have needed stronger evidence of her husband's adultery, or Louis would have had to admit to the act in court.

If Martha pressed the issue, she may have brought great embarrassment to the family and caused herself to be seen as the homewrecker. This may have ruined her chances at maintaining parental rights to see her only living child. Her only hope, if she wanted to stay in Ralph's life, was to stay married.

3. Perfumed Kindness.

She sent perfumed kindness to people she thought blind.

Deceit behind that scent,

She thought I would not find.

You're not too old to punish.

You cannot do wrong and feel right.

You can cheat the weak and helpless

But not fool the one of *Almight*.

Editorial Comments

The perfumed item sent is a reference to the letter Martha received addressed to Louis from his lady friend, as described in the poem, "The Ballad of Martha." Her comment about fooling those around may be in reference to how Louis said he would never admit to having an affair. It also remains possible that Martha blew the evidence out of proportion.

4. Bitterness.

Kiss her with the sweetness of your lips,

for your kisses are sweeter than wine,

to wash away the bitterness,

that is, on lips of mine.

Editorial Comments

Martha's and mocking response to an alleged affair is not addressed to anyone, nor are several other of her more embittered writings. One might conclude these notes were never sent. It would certainly not behoove Martha to share her worst thoughts on paper with the man she also depended on to obtain her release.

Illustration 24: Mr. and Mrs. Louis Nasch Jr. on their honeymoon.

Credit: Unknown postcard photographer. Courtesy of Ralph Nasch.

5. "Forbidden Lust"

In a little country dwelling, in a rugged Northern space,

With Jackpines, lakes, and hillocks surrounding the dear place,

Lives a little, gray-haired mother, so wrinkled and so old.

Her sympathizing love and ways, to her children, she is gold.

When they have grief and sorrows, to her they will complain.

She knows just how to comfort them, though her own heart beats pain.

Her daughter from a city, a place so grand and gay,

Went to this dear, old mother, to that lonely place to stay.

Misfortune overtook her and marred her choice in life,

When the dearest one she had on earth was unfaithful to his wife.

She told her dear, old mother, "On earth there is none so true

Who feels my grief and sorrows with aching heart, like you."

[cont.]

In that isolated country, they talked of courtship days,

Soon, visions appeared: thoughts of her sweetheart's caressing ways.

With the little love that lingered within her lonely heart,

She shared how romance ended and how they were forced to part.

She doubted if this would stay true. It seems more like a dream,

When thoughts drift back to bygone days. How real his love then seemed.

How could he wrong his faithful mate? In him, her heart did trust.

How could he wreck her home and life for God's forbidden lust!

6. Failure.

Someday, your heart will be broken

                like mine.

And by your failure,

            you'll see,

When from grief and sorrow, you'll choken

        and pine.

Your thoughts, then, will drift back

    to me.

Burning regret, to you, will come

and you'll wish you were my mate.

But wishes, Dear, no more will count,

for then, it will be

too late.

7. Unfaithful.

Fond memories of courtship days when I sat upon your knee.
You put your arms around me, Dear, and whispered love to me.

In happiness, we soon did wed. Our future seemed so wide,
When temptation stole into our home and wrecked you at my side.

My heart was pierced by grief and my eyes were blurred and wet.
The suffering that you have caused, I never can forget.

You cried and asked me to forgive and take you back once more,
That you would promise to be good and never leave my door.

I will forgive and with you live, as it's so hard to part.
I'll try and help you to go straight with a crooked, broken heart.

Editorial Comments

The door metaphor appears in her writing in several occasions to indicate being
where people enter into or exit a relationship.

8. Broken Romance.

There is snow upon the mountains,

        There is sand upon the plain,

But the grief that's in my heart, Dear,

        I never can full explain.

I am longing for your friendship.

For your pleasant smile, I yearn.

If you only knew my heartache,

Back to me, you would return.

Once, you told me that you loved me

And we named our wedding day.

        Then, you chose another sweetheart

        And with me, you would not stay.

[cont.]

Now, I sit here in my cabin

And I'm feeling oh, so blue.

I think back on our sweet romance,

When you promised to be true.

Oft, I held your hands in mine, Dear,

As we parted at your door.

Now, I sit here sad and weeping

On the dark and lonely shore.

In my dreams, I try to claim you

And I call you "All My Own."

As I awake,

I am forsaken:

I find myself

Alone.

9. "Your Dreams"

Written from Louis Jr.'s point of view.

I dreamed a beautiful scene

In a mossy valley so deep.

Ripp'ling streams are flowing,

Evergreens are growing,

And lush vines of ivy do creep.

By that stream, she appeared to me.

I knew in my gut she was nigh.

I thought she was calling,

I felt myself falling,

Then I woke with tremb'ling sigh.

How disappointing, what I'd seen.

Love dreams can only be so vain.

I wish they were more real.

How happy I would feel.

To be released of my heart's pain.

II: My Husband, For One

10. Ballad of Louis.

Written from Louis Jr.'s point of view.

When I was but a little waif,

My mother did not stay.

She only lived six months with me

And then she passed away.

Then, my grandma took me

And raised me at her side.

For seven years I had a home.

I was her joy and pride.

Then, my father reclaimed me,

And took me to his home.

And there, I found my stepmother

Who had a heart of stone.

In constant torment, I did dwell.

My eyes were filled with tears.

I had none but a prison cell,

For over ten long years.

[cont.]

Back to my grandma, I did go,

To cheer her lonely life —

To help in every way I know

Through struggles and through strife.

I felt so happy and so free

And felt I had a home,

When grandma passed away from me

And left me all alone.

From then, I was left forsaken.

I did not care for life

Until when I met a maiden

And she became my wife.

Editorial Comments

Originally titled "Life of Louis." Louis Jr.'s grandmother, Mary Kahles died in 1911, but he and Martha had been dating since 1909. The poem does not accurately reflect this sequence.

11. Courtship Days.

Sweet memories of courtship days, when love was young and dear,

True messages of your kind ways were music to my ears.

When days were warm and nights were cool, we strolled both hand in hand

To those steps of Jefferson School — the place we thought so grand.

You spoke to me so tenderly, your lips were sweet and true.

I felt your heart belonged to me and mine belonged to you.

How sad our romantic end is, whence we lived together.

Love was changed to darkness and in came stormy weather.

Why was your God so cruel to us to let you go and stray?

Instead of binding love for us, he took that gift away.

Are you sad since I am locked in? To see an empty chair?

Or am I now long gone, forgotten? For me, you no more care?

Editorial Comments

The Jefferson School in mention is a "secondary" school located at the intersection of Western Ave. S. and West Sturgis St. in downtown St. Paul. It was approximately two miles from the Nasch home at 642 Hall Avenue.

The stormy weather reference is later repeated in the poem "A Bride" as a word of warning to a newlywed. The empty chair metaphor is used as a reference to a missing person.

12. Cottage.

To Louis.

There is a little cottage–

of it, I one time knew.

Surrounding it are trees and vines

and flowers – every hue.

Within this little cottage,

a hero and his son,

must struggle on in lonely strife

until their tasks are done.

This precious little cottage,

once dear to me and you –

When Ralph came in, I was cast out.

There left just room for two.

[cont.]

Did I even have a mother?

What did she think or do

to birth out such a condemned freak

of whom God never knew.

Editorial Comments

Martha's final four lines reflect the pseudoscience belief that a mother's sin (including sinful thoughts or intentions) could influence the prenatal development of a child, up to and including an early termination or stillbirth, based on the severity of the mother's condition. Here, Martha laments that her mental health situation may be a generational curse, passed down because of something her mother must have done.

13. Home.

To Louis. 1932.

A lovely thatched cottage sitting on hill, high—
Its model: old-fashioned: so humble to eye.
For thirteen brief years, in that box, I did roam.
To me, it was precious—that dear, little home.

The trees and the flowers were lovely to see.
The garden was cherished by you and by me.
We sat in the swing with young Ralph at our side.
That dear little pet was our joy and pride.

Our pictures still linger, and all that we have
Brings memories of wedlock that ended so sad.
Deserted and lonely, you struggle in strife,
And I, claimed by devil, who ended my life.

Suffering in agony, ever I roam,
For no more to see the place I called home.
The world, which has vanished right out of my sight,
Was changed into darkness, as if it were night.

14. The Blue For-Get-Me-Not.

To Louis.

You raise flowers of every hue
The Rose, Iris, and Larkspur blue...
But there's one missing on your lot:
It is the pale blue For-Get-Me-Not.
If, in my honor, you will plant
This little flower, blue,
And change its name to "Memories —
When I was once with you."

Once, I had a life like flowers
And thrived upon the land.
And then, I was destroyed to naught
By strong and mighty hand.
I was changed into a thistle
And rooted out, unsoiled.
And now, I am thought much less
Than dry burrs on sand, untoiled.
No one cares for a worthless weed.
By sickle, it must fall:
Be cast into an unknown place,
Forgotten then, by all.

15. Memories.

To Louis. 1932.

Give me something to remember you by, since we were forced to part—

A kiss or two, imprinted by you, forever to remain in my heart.

I do recall the eve that we met. It was in September, you know, at a Labor

Day ball at Hiawatha Hall, just twenty-three years ago. Four years later,

in wedlock, we joined, but our romance would not do well. Then the devil

stepped in with the whole world's sin and took me off to hell.

He led me away, forever to stay

behind prison bars and keys.

In agony, I squirm

like a suffering worm

and beg for mercy on my knees.

I'm judged as a goof and a nut, and classed far less than a mule.

Behind thickened walls, where Satan now calls, I play the asylum fool.

Editorial Comments

The Hiawatha Dance Hall was called the Hiawatha Temple and was located at 500 Wabasha St. in St. Paul, Minnesota. The Foxtrot dance style was popular at this time because ofVernon and Irene Castle - celebrity dancers featured on Broadway, vaudeville and in motion pictures. Curiously, Martha's detail about meeting Louis Jr. for the first time at a dance hall does not match Louis Jr.'s recollection of meeting at the dairy-creamery near the Gruening farm.

The similarities between poems "Memories" and "Home," suggest both may have been written in or around an anniversary time. Here, the reference to meeting twenty-three years prior, leads researchers to September 6, 1909, which gives the poem a date in 1932. In "Home," the dates in reference are misleading because they lead from the point of cohabitation (1913) to a future date of her mental health collapse which appears to be in either 1926 or 27, per her calculations.

16. A Castle.

To Louis.

You
Have a little castle.
It stands up on a hill.
Its color:
Green, a pretty scene
To bring a home-like thrill.
In its rooms,
You
Cozy, dwell
In comfort, but forlorn to know that
You,
Alone,
Must be,
And live,
As if in mourn.

I'm gone
But not forgotten
By you,
Nor by your pet.
The memories of this Mamma, you can't and won't forget.

[cont.]

You
Gaze at your only child when he is at his play,
To know
That he
Is motherless
And left alone to stray.

You
Must ignore that
Ever
I shared
Your little home.
Put all your love into our child,
As onward,
You
Must roam.

You think
If there were a way
For you to change that life,
To get back
To the bygone days
When I was once your wife,

[cont.]

If you knew
My
Agony,
Your heartaches
Would not
Cease.
They'd haunt you in your weakest —-
You'd sink
Upon your knees.

If you knew
There is no way,
There is no chance,
Nor hope,
You'd want to end those horrid thoughts –
To hang
Up
On a rope.

Editorial Comments

This poem uses the same 7-6-8-6 quatrain meter as found in "Life in Northern Pines," "A Mother's Ways," and "Imprisoned." (**See Maps for a street view of the house.**)

17. Son In Need.

To Louis.

Do you sometimes of me think

That, in chain of heavy link,

I am bound right to the cross

And from the earth I am lost?

Is your son the one you love

Better than the stars above?

He will never do you wrong,

As to him, you do belong.

He will seek you everywhere.

He will need your tender care.

He will hear you when you call

And will help you when you fall.

[cont.]

What would life without him be?

When you sit and think of me,

When your eyes are blurred and wet,

He will help you to forget.

He will say, "Oh, Daddy Dear,

Wipe away your lonely tears."

He will smooth the rugged way,

And he'll take your gloom away.

When you feel you are alone,

He will cheer your lonely home.

When you're longing for a friend,

He'll be faithful to the end.

When your earthly strife is o'er

And you're anchored on that shore,

You will call to him in lack,

Try to follow in my track.

Editorial Comments

The "track" expression appears in other poems to mean a way of doing something, or an example. One can guess here that Martha is suggesting Louis Jr. either follows her example, or sets a good example for Ralph.

Stanza three contains two expressions also found in the old hymn, "Oh, the Best Friend to have is Jesus," by Peter Philip Billhorn in 1891. The lyrics and a piano soundtrack are available through the BlueLetterBible.org.

18. Forsaken.

To Louis. 1929.

When it's Springtime in the valley,
And it's Fall out on the sea,
And you think of coming pleasure,
Do you sometimes think of me?

Do you think of our dear courtship
That was twenty years ago,
When you called me "Dear" and "Sweetheart,"
And you were my only beau?

When at eve, at golden sunset,
Hand in hand, we used to roam.
And we spoke of our great future,
Now laid wrecked beneath the foam.

All alone, I lie forsaken,
And you do not hear me scream
In my everlasting *toarcher*,
While, in peace, you lie and dream.

Have I messed your life forever?
Am I now where I belong,
In this dark and haunted *barrok*,
For I've done the world great wrong?

Editorial Comments

In the final stanza, Martha reveals her feelings on being unjustly criminalized.

Based on the twenty year remark, this poem was written in approximately 1929. Stanza three contains a reflection from an 1897, Book of the Royal Blue, published by the Baltimore and Ohio Railroad Company's passenger dept. This variety magazine was provided to passengers free of charge as a form of en route entertainment. On page 129, the text reads:

> *The Days That Are.*
> *Jerome P. Fleishman*
>
> *When I was young I used to write about the days gone by, And in my verse I used to sling full many a love-sick sigh; I used to write about the shady dell and rippling stream, And yearn in four-line spasms for the olden loves young dream. I used to pen a verse or two about the days of yore, And sometimes tell about the love that lives for evermore; I'd wander into pastures green and many meadows fair, And chase my love-lorn fancy through the scented evening air.*
> *A trysting place, I sang about, **and told of golden hours, When, hand in hand, we used to roam** among the dew-kissed flowers. Imploring eyes and glances shy, I rang in good and free, And wrote in metric flights of days when we would happy be.*

This Fleishman poem continues to discuss how the romance fades when instead of trotting on an outing with one's lover, the author was trotting to the nursery to attend to a baby's diaper.

19. A Cottonwood Tree.

A cottonwood tree with large boughs hung

Where many a songbird's nest have swung

Upon your hill, with lovely grace,

For many years have marked that place.

Those pretty leaves, now turning to gold,

Are spreading the news of coming cold.

Soon, these leaves will soft flutter down,

Covering grass in *carpit,* brown.

I've raked those leaves for many a year.

It was a pleasure I loved so dear.

I did not know how soon *'twould* be

That I would fall like leaves of tree.

[cont.]

Beneath that tree, we oft' times sat

And spoke of strife and woe.

We did not know how soon *'twould* be

That I would have to go:

To have no world, nor loved ones near,

All nature's beauty marred.

To be cast into hell, alive,

And in an asylum, barred.

If I'd have known this suffering,

I'd have climbed into that tree

To jump right headlong into space,

To break my neck in three.

For years and years, I shed my tears

And wept my life away.

I felt that curse upon my soul

For sins of world to pay.   [cont.]

Some memories make you happy.

Others can turn you blue.

But those few of home and loved ones,

I cannot share with you.

I was robbed of home and freedom,

From husband, child, and kin.

I was cursed and damned by Satan

To suffer the world's sin!

Editorial Comments

The cottonwood tree mentioned here becomes a point of grim focus in "A Painter." It may have also been where a bench swing was strung, as referenced in "Home." (See Map 4 for a street view of the house.)

There is a structural shift in the meter and rhyme scheme after the first stanza. This may indicate writing in multiple stages or a sudden emotional change.

20. A Painter.

To Louis.

1. A painter stands bewildered and sighs a heavy sob.
    He knows he has no money and not a sign of job.

2. Bills are heaped upon him, his taxers are in the near,
    He needs to buy more coal if to warm him in winter's drear.

3. His little home not payed for, a mortgage he must meet.
    If, in this, he fails, he'll be cast into the street.

4. He is alone without a mate, his young child to rear.
    With all burdens heaped on him, he lives in constant fear.

5. His first thoughts in the morning are how to make ends meet,
    Or how to dodge the debtor when passing on the street.

6. He is so over burdened from worry and from grief,
    And thinking if he must go out and be a wicked thief.

7. He does not want to break the laws of God, nor man.
    He *tryes* to find relief and hope the best ways that he can.

8. How hard I *tryed* to help him with all the strength I had.
    The devil came, destroyed my life, and made his oh, so sad!

9. If he knew my suffering, he'd climb the highest mound
    To jump headlong into space, to smash upon the ground.

21. Somewhere.

To Louis.

Somewhere, the sun is shining.

Somewhere, a little rain.

Somewhere, a heart is pining

For me, but all in vain.

Someone is sad and lonely.

Someone is feeling blue.

If I am not mistaken,

Tell me, Dear, it it you?

Someone whom you do worship

Has destroyed my soul and life,

And changed your home to sadness

To live without a wife.

[cont.]

All burdens now heap on you.

You must bear a heavy lot.

You have no mate to share them,

As on through life you *throad*.

Someday, I'll be deserted

When more loved ones are all gone,

When everyone I knew here

Has entered home beyond.

Someday, a dying hero,

You, will send your last farewell

To me, who's left behind you,

Forever in this hell.

Editorial Comments

The first stanza appears remarkably similar to the chorus in a Charles K. Harris song, "Somewhere," from 1906. The full chorus reads:

> *Somewhere the sun is shining,*
> *Somewhere a little rain,*
> *Somewhere a heart is pining,*
> *For love but all in vain,*
>
> *Somewhere a soul is drifting,*
> *Further and far apart,*
> *Somewhere my love lies dreaming,*
> *Somewhere, a broken heart.*

22 and 23. He Said, She Said

Unhappy Home.	Happy Home.

7	Our home was never happy.	It takes a heap of living
6	We never could agree.	To make a happy home.
8	I wished that something would occur	Without the love of little ones,
6	To set me once more free.	You feel you are alone.

7	The devil came and got her	They are gifts of God to you.
6	And put her in a cell.	Their love is so sincere.
7	Forever she must suffer	When you are sad and weary,
6	And be alive in hell.	They brighten you with cheer.

8	I have a darling little son.	You're longing to see their future.
6	He's all the world to me.	You plan for them each day,
8	He covers up my darkened life,	For dreams they may possess in life
6	For never more to see.	To come, in easy way.

8	A bachelor life we now enjoy.	When you are in a feeble age,
6	We do what we like best.	For you, they will provide,
8	We have no one around to nag,	And help you every way they can,
6	Disturbing peaceful rest.	And keep you at their side.

7	When my earthly tasks are done,	When your earthly strife is o'er
6	And I am called by God,	And you are called beyond,
7	I hope I may rest in peace	By then, all's left behind you;
6	When I'm beneath the sod.	Your name will still pass on.

Editorial Comments

Meter marks have been added intentionally to show the match between these two poems. Though they are structured alike, the tone of "Unhappy Home" (originally left untitled), written in Louis's perspective, is noticeably selfish and short-sighted, while "Happy Home," written in Martha's perspective, is much more selfless and future-oriented.

24. The Golden West.

To Louis.

You always longed for the Golden West.

Was there, you wished to be.

But all your longings, now, have been wrecked.

All, on account of me.

Editorial Comments

Louis's half-siblings eventually relocated from Minnesota to California (**see Family Trees**). Perhaps this was Louis Jr.'s desire as well, but Martha's confinement interfered with his plans.

25. The Coat.

Louis sent an old plush coat for me to wear as a sweater and told me not to discard it — that he wanted it back, if I did not want it. This is my answer to his suggestion:

That patched up plush coat, a sight to human eyes. Why worry I will part with it? You must value it as prize. Who would want that worn-out frock which is now green and old? The dumbest goof would not wear it if they were numb with cold! I got that coat to keep me warm from winter winds and snow. I felt its comfort at that time, eighteen years ago. I traveled the world and felt alive when that coat was brand new. I was home with a mate whom I loved dear and true.

Do not think you will see the remains of this coat. It would last longer put on a worthless goat. I lie around on a hard bench from morning until night. There is no chance to wear it out, or even put it out of my sight. But — if you desire the tired item, which you consider so dear, I'll send it back, at your request, to save as a souvenir.

124

Editorial Comments

The eighteen year reference leads back to a time frame between 1910 and 1914.
Martha's mention that it was new at a time when she was wed, narrows this range
to 1913-1914. This results in this poem being written in either 1931 or 1932.

III: Our Child, A Pawn

26. Pretty Boy.

To Ralph.

There are boys that are witty, there are some that are true,
But the one that is pretty is the one that is you.

Your form is so handsome, your face is so fair,
Your arms, so strong, Son, you've well fragranced your hair.

Your charm is so taking and your smile is so sweet,
You'll surely be raking to all people you meet.

Your friends will like you, surely inviting when they can.
Beware Temptation's luring when you become a man.

Always do as Daddy says, hearken to his call.
He will know the smoothest ways so you will not fall.

Always be a heart winner, let scandal pass you by,
For you are not a sinner, you'll hold your head up high.

Editorial Comments

Ralph Louis Nasch was born November 15, 1921 at West Side General Hospital and baptized January 1, 1922 at the West Side Old Emmanuel Lutheran Church.

The reference to pains of cutting knife could be metaphorical and suggest a great deal of pain, as Ralph's official birth record does not indicated birth by cesarean. Curiously, in Louis Jr.'s letters to Ralph, he said Martha had to stay in the hospital two weeks after the birth, due to it being considered difficult and "being your mother was up in age when she went thru this."

Illustration 25: July 1926. "Ralph 4 years, 8 mo. old with a sober look and a bauke [bouquet] of flowers in his right hand. Allwis [Always] shows our outside wash post and the open big barn door and house. The living room window."

Credit: Louis Nasch Jr. Courtesy of Janelle Molony.

27. Ralph.

I know a little youngster;
The top choice of his school.
He is polite and modest
And follows Golden Rule.

His perfect class attendance
Each day of the school year,
Has won him certificates
And brought to him good cheer.

He is the joy and sunshine.
Of his dear father's heart.
He is the pride and favored
Of teachers in his art.

His eyes are bright and hazel,
His lips are like a rose.
He's getting more romantic,
As up in life he grows.

When he grows into a man,
For Daddy, he'll provide,
And help every way he can,
And stay right by his side.

Editorial Comments

Ralph Nasch attended Garfield School at George St. E. and Gorman Ave. The school was a quarter-mile from his home and would have taken him about eight minutes to walk there. As his retelling goes, he walked uphill in the snow, both ways, to get there and back.

Ralph's eye color was actually a light blue, not to be confused with green whatsoever. This error could indicate Martha having difficulty remembering her son's face.

Illustration 26:
September 12, 1927. The caption on the reverse reads: "Ralph, 5 years, 9 mo. 3 weeks old. ...at the old homestead. Mother had her apraction [operation] at that time all ready."

Louis Jr. recalled that a nearby neighbor, Mrs. Schafer, "took Ralph and George down to Garfield School on their first day ... Ralph, Mother had an operation June 8 1927 and was too weak to take you" (1957).

In the background, is the two-seater outhouse. The Nasches did not have indoor plumbing until 1934. The family sponge-bathed once per week and sometimes showered at the downtown YMCA.

Credit: Louis or Martha Nasch. Courtesy Janelle Molony.

28. Perfect Dad.

To Ralph.

Written from Ralph's point of view.

My daddy is a perfect man.
He's always kind to me.
He helps me every way he can.
My faults, he does not see.

He helps me in the morning.
When everything seems wrong,
He lifts my little burdens,
Puts things where they belong.

He plays with me, just like a child.
He's never rude, nor bold.
I wish he'd always stay like that
And never would grow old.

What would I do without him?
Where would I go or stay?
When I am most discouraged,
He always finds a way.

Illustration 27: June 2, 1929.

"Ralph 7 years, 6 ½ mo. old. Ralph is a sherf [sic]. Got his star on and the big hat with tasels [sic] with a nice little smile and his tent by our homestead. Pa took all the pictures."

In a photo from the same day, Louis wrote, "If you look close, he has his lasoo [sic] rope twisted around his waist line and his gun."

In Ralph's reminiscence, he wrote: "When we didn't play at my home, we would go to the 'woods,' about two blocks away, where there were hills and trees. Here, we would play hide and seek and our favorite pastime of those days... 'Cowboys and Indians' ... chasing each other with rubber binder guns that we made ourselves (*A Grandfather Remembers*, 1987.)

Credit: Louis J. Nasch Jr. Courtesy of Janelle Molony.

29. *Advized* By Dad.

To Ralph.

Written from Louis Jr.'s point of view.

I would not become a painter for all the fabled gold—to be
remembered for a while, forgotten when you're old—to always have to
be at some contractor's beck and call—to have to kiss him for a job
that you don't like at all… When summer days are bright and clear,
they call for you to come. When winter days are cold and drear, you're
nothing but a bum!

I did not have the chance you have, to be *advized* by Dad.
Mine did not seem to care for me, if I were glad or sad.

I want you to choose a better way for when you get old, so you
do not have to kiss the boss and march as you are told. You want to be
an artist—to paint in vivid blue and white—to have the public speak
of you, that you are *verry* bright! You'll paint a scene of moonlight:
it's softly sparkling in a stream, with pretty mermaids, of course, who
pose for your evening dream.

30. Babe O-Mine.

To Ralph.

Two pretty little baby feet that once were mine, so warm and sweet. I harbored them beneath my heart and now we, too, must live apart.

Two precious little baby hands, so tender and so white. When I would put you in your bed they'd wave at me, "Good night." Your eyes, then, were bright and Hazel, and you had such flaxy hair. Your little lips would softly speak that familiar bedtime prayer.

Your daddy saved your little shoes and he also saved your cap to remind him of baby days, when you sat upon his lap. The memories of Mamma, though, you cannot eas'ly recall, as you were in such tender age when I had to leave you all.

Editorial Comments

Martha's final line about Ralph not being able to remember his younger days is echoed in "Little Boy Blues."

Illustration 28: Ralph Louis Nasch (November 15, 1921 - November 23, 2019), pictured at twelve months old.

Credit: Foreseen Studio, Hamm Bldg. St. Paul, Minn. Courtesy of Ralph Nasch

31. Ralph's Dandelions.

To Ralph.

When Ralph was only two years old, he came in from the grass.
In his hands, some dandelions, "Mamma, put these in a vase?"

Those memories, I can't forget. They haunt me day and night.
How sweet of such a darling pet to be so smart and bright.

How ripe the sound of "Mamma" that echoes in my ears.
Now, Satan tries to destroy it for never more to hear.

He was so frail and delicate. His tiny hands, so weak.
His little voice, so baby-like, so tender, and so meek.

I hope to God it pleased my child to get for him, a glass,
To put in it, this yellow gift found growing in the grass.

Illustration 29: July 30, 1926. "Ralph 4 years, 8 ½ mo. L. 42, M. 36. The next year, July 1927, Mama had her operation." Ralph may be looking at an Alstroemeria plant.

About the garden, Ralph wrote, "In my early years, my friends and I played a lot in our yard because it was probably the largest in the neighborhood. My father kept it very nice and worked hard to make it attractive to all visitors. He would often scold me and my friends if we did any damage to plants, shrubs, or the vegetable garden" (*A Grandfather Remembers*, 1987).

Credit: Louis Nasch Jr. Courtesy of Janelle Molony.

32. A Scholar.

My Ralph is quite a scholar. He likes to read and write.

He goes to school in daytime and *studdies* books at night.

He always is so thrifty. He *tryes* his *verry* best.

The teacher thinks him nifty to be beyond the rest.

He also helps his daddy in every way he can.

He wants to be a master when he becomes a man.

Politeness is his motto. He is a perfect boy.

Daddy is so proud of him. He is his pride and joy.

How would he do without Ralph, now that he's left alone?

He must have love and comfort to share his lonely home.

33. A Prayer.

A notation on the top of the page reads: "I composed for Ralph. It means nothing to me…"

Come, dear Lord, and hold my hands

And teach me how to pray,

So I may see a better land

From you, I cannot stray.

Give me my health, brightness in mind,

So of some use, I'll be—

To help the weaker ones along,

To lead them on to thee.

If Satan wants to tempt me

Spread out your wings so wide

That I may seek for shelter

And from his clutches, slide.

Be my guide and comfort

Whenever I may go.

The ways that lead to safety,

Without you, I don't know.

If I may follow in your track,

Regret will not be known.

It will lead me to a place on high

Where *Paradize* is shown.   Amen.

34. "Little Boy Blues"

At a party for little boys,

They sang the song of "Home, Sweet Home,"

But one little boy just looked on.

He knew they all had a Mamma.

He could not recall when he had,

Welled up with tears his eyes had drawn.

He felt lonely, walked away,

And sat right down by the wayside—

For a little while he would stay.

He sang a song all of his own,

Out where no one else could hear him.

He sang to remember those days.

[cont.]

"If I only had a Mamma,

Then I'd live in a Home, Sweet Home

Like all the rest of little boys.

Daddy tells me of baby days,

When Mamma was here at our side.

Back then, my world must have held joys.

But I don't remember that time—

Not even the smallest ember.

My daddy tries to keep the spark.

She must be worried about us.

My daddy is all I have left,

Since when she was forced to depart."

Editorial Comments

This poem may have been influenced by a 1906 song, "If Only I Had a Home Sweet Home," by J. Johns. The main character in John's lyrics is a little orphan boy on the street, looking into the window of a home (supposedly hosting a party with boys). Some of the lyrics read:

VERSE 1:
'Twas a party for the little ones,/ And ere they all could go,/ They sang the song of "Home, Sweet Home,"/ The one we all love so,/ without, a ragged child looked on,/ His heart so lone and sad,/ He never had a home, sweet home,/ 'Mid sobs and tears he said:

CHORUS:
If I only had a home, sweet home,/ Someone to care for me,/ Like all the other boys and girls,/ How happy I would be;/ A kind papa and a mama dear/ To call me all their own,/ This world would be all sunshine/ if I had a home, sweet home.

Originally titled "Blues," this poem was the first poem that appears at the beginning of the book, on the reverse side pages.

35. "Ralph's Plea"

Written from Ralph's point of view.

Daddy Dear, I want my Mamma.
Why'd you let law take her away?
For you knew I loved her dearly
And want her home with me to stay!

Every day, for her, I'm longing,
Each night, for her, I softly pray.
If she knew that we are lonely,
Surely she'd kiss our tears away.

As your child, I'll try to lead you,
Lead you gently on a father's way.
And with kindness, I shall teach you
How to be more loving, every day.

I will draw you closer together,
So you will never want to stray.
I shall bind you both with my own love,
If you'd only bring her home to stay.

[cont.]

Every letter we get from Mamma,

She says that evil took her away.

If only we could help her get free

From what terrible sins she must pay.

Editorial Comments

This poem provides evidence that Martha did not self-admit to the hospital. The fourth stanza suggests Martha believes her marriage (or at least the appearances of such) is salvageable, if only for Ralph's sake.

There are a few unique mechanical features shown including how the meter gradually increases. Stanzas one and two use eight syllable lines, stanza three alternates eight and nine syllables, then the final two stanzas keep nine syllables in each. Her final line is a reprise from "A Cottonwood Tree."

IV: So, Here I Rot

36. Suffering.

I stand at the bar of justice,
A creature wan and wild.
I'm formed as if a woman,
But helpless as a child.

A worn down look of sorrow
Is etched into my face,
For everlasting suffering
Has left that silent trace.

I was led astray by Satan
And led right into hell,
Where you no more can help me,
My dearest ones. Farewell.

How dark and tasteless the hours
When Jesus, no longer I see.
All sweetness that is heaped on you
Is changing to wormwood for me.

Editorial Comments

This is the first time Martha uses a direct name for her spiritual oppressor, instead of "devil" or other evil personification. In Biblical references, wormwood is a bitter herb that could be used in small quantities as an antiparasitic. When consumed in larger quantities, death resulted.

The first two stanzas are a reiteration of a poem published in 1904 titled, "Guilty, or Not Guilty" by an anonymous author. Their lines read: "SHE stood at the bar of justice, A creature wan and wild, In form too small for a woman, In feature too old for a child. For a look so worn and pathetic, Was stamped on her pale young face, It seemed long years of suffering Must have left that silent trace."

(Source: Bliss Carman, et al., eds. The World's Best Poetry. Volume III. Sorrow and Consolation. 1904. https://www.bartleby.com/360/3/122.html)

The inclusion of these ideas may have been commentary on the current legal state of affairs that keep Martha as a dependant of her husband's (or male next of kin's) guardianship, without a opportunity to speak on her own behalf – possibly having no ability to consent to or refuse various medical treatments (or experiments) or other "alternative" methods for reforming inmates.

The final stanza is a reiteration of a 1779 poem by hymnist John Newton (1725-1807) titled, "None upon Earth I Desire Beside Thee," where he writes: "How tedious and tasteless the hours, When Jesus no longer I see! Sweet prospects, sweet birds, and sweet flow'rs, Have lost all their sweetness to me."

(Source: *The Works of John Newton*, Vol. 3, 358. Or From Olney Hymns (1779), Book I)

37. The Asylum.

Written for a patient, by request.

What is human life to us,

when in this Asylum,

we must be away from home and every place,

for never more to see.

See!

We have no future to look for!

We have no past to recall!

Life, in here, is changed to naught, where darkness… covers all.

We sit so lonely. Our eyes are blurred and wet...

for days,

for months,

and years,

just waiting…

We're waiting for our death.

[cont.]

If, from this place, we were released,

we'd wander in disgrace,

for all our friends would fear us,

since being in this place.

In this place,

like a factory,

they come in day-by-day.

Some of them—restored to health within an easy way.

Some are much too violent—they rave and rant around.

To keep them under control—in camisole are bound.

Some are a total wreck—put in this place to stay.

They do not know they are alive—have not a word to say.

From being in a place like this, of what you have to see…

If (you're) not insane when coming in,

it won't be long…

you'll be.

Editorial Comments

The camisole in reference is a half-body (upper body) restraint that kept both arms crossed in front of the body, and it was secured by buckles in the back.

INSANE HOSPITAL, ST. PETER, MINN.

Illustration 30: Insane Hospital, St. Peter, Minn. Lithographic Found in "Illustrated historical atlas of the State of Minnesota. 1874" (U.S. Atlas) p. 69.

Credit: A.T. Andreas (1939-1900). From David Rumsey Historical Map Collection.

38. Too Poor For Freedom.

Written for a patient, by request.

It is a crime and sorrow to be away from home,

for children there, who need my care,

are now left all alone.

I was brought here with no chance, without a word to say.

I am now in perfect health—I need no longer stay!

I want my home and freedom.

My children need my care!

For they are sad and lonely and long to see me there.

My daughter, in tender age, must be more like mother,

to try to earn a living for sister and her brother.

They, now, are left as orphans.

Their father: two years dead.

I must go back to help them to earn their daily bread.

Is anyone interested? Anyone at all…

in now setting me free,

so I may go home to them

and be at liberty?

Editorial Comments

Originally titled "Freedom."
In both poems #38 "Too Poor..." and #40 "Imprisoned," Martha craves liberty
and affirms that patients were kept in the hospital against their will, even when in
perfect health. In "The Asylum," she hints at others coming into the hospital with
no disability or mental illness that she could observe, though she has no medical
expertise to say so.

In another patient's account from St. Peter's Hospital, Alice B. Russell wrote,
"People are sometimes driven insane by treatment and despair in the hospital ...
Some people are kept there who are no more insane than the people who send
them, and should be at liberty" (*A Plea for the Insane,* 1898, Roberts Publishing
Co: Minneapolis, MN).

After one short period of confinement in 1883, Alice B. Russell advocated for
hospital reform through writing hers and other patient's stories. She returned for a
second, three-year committal from 1903-1906.

39. Outcast.

A lush garden, once mine, on top of a mound

With fruit trees and bushes and vines spread around,

With shade trees and shrubbery, and flowers so fair:

A small, ancient cottage, so humble and rare.

I lived in this cottage for many long years.

My life there was nothing but sorrow and tears.

I had none but hardship, with struggles and strife.

I was but an outcast, each day of my life.

The neighbors all shunned me and sneered in my face.

I felt they were crowding me off of that place.

The devil entered in to finish his game,

My whole world to destroy and cast into shame.

He put me in *toarcher*, forever to roam,

And stole me away from the place I called home.

In dark, haunted guardhouse, I'm placed in a cell

To live, forever alive, in my hell.

Editorial Comments

In reference to stanza four's "cell:"
This description of a guardhouse or cell may either be hyperbole, or may indicate that at some point, Martha was kept in a barred room as if a prisoner. She has elsewhere mentioned being in a barracks.

Regarding her use of the word "torture:"
While it is nearly impossible to say what Martha considered torture, some common therapies included the applicaiton of leeches (blood letting or thinning), injection or ingestion of mercury or other mild toxins, freezing cold baths, and internal cleanses (enemas and douches). Patients with illnesses affecting their appetite were force fed, with or without a light sedation. A patient's progress and determination for discharge relied heavily on their cooperation with these and other treatments. A rebellious or disobedient patient could expect to have their treatment plan extended.

Regarding if the hospital was "haunted:"
Some people who have been in the hospital believe that it was and still is haunted. Prior to 2020, staff members of the St. Peter State Hospital reported the facility as "haunted" to an investigator with MinnesotaGhosts.com. The paranormal investigators reported the following:

> "Staff members have heard voices calling out to them and screaming in the underground tunnels that connect the buildings…" Many inmates have used the tunnels to try an escape into the farm fields. Rumor says the tunnels may have been too confusing and people became lost, and eventually perished. Other staff reported seeing human-figured shadows in the hallways, and everyone the MPSG spoke to agreed the hospital "has unseen patients that still reside there."

The website for the Minnesota Paranormal Sightings Group (MinnesotaGhosts.com) has since been taken down with the owner's retirement, but another leading area ghosthunter, John Savage of Minnesota Paranormal Investigators, suspects that St. Peter State Hospital stalls new investigations "because of the things that have happened to others that they don't want known to the public" (2021, October 18, Personal communication to Janelle Molony).

40. Imprisoned.

You have a home so cozy,
Someone to love you, too.
The world is oh, so big and wide.
It all belongs to you.

You wake up in the morning
And see the sun so grand.
You know you are at liberty
And need not heed command.

You go out in the open.
Give thanks on bended knees
That you are not a prisoner.
You hear no chimes of keys!

But why was I forsaken?
Why was I born so odd?
To have no world to be in—
No home, no friend, nor God.

41. Mary.

Every day she flops around with shoes three sizes too big. She's dolled up in

the prison garb and thinks it is time to gig. She bosses all the patients around

and forces them to eat and when they cannot swallow putrid soup,

she pokes

down

hunks of meat.

She grabs them poor saps by the neck. Her fists almost knock them out.

When her commands they do not heed, such, to open up their mouth, she

yanks them down onto a bench and forces their jaw unset.

She rips

their clothes

right off their backs

when they have soaked them all wet.

She is so over willing to do as some nurses will say!

She wants so hard to please the staff in her sick and cunning way!

What would nurses do without her? For to manage all us goofs...

If it wasn't for Mary Peterson and her

very

heavy hoofs.

Editorial Comments

We have attempted to identify a Mary Peterson and have found the following:

Multiple Mary Petersons lived in St. Paul, Minnesota in the 1920s-30s. Multiple Mary Petersons were logged in the asylum's casebook near to the time of Martha's stay. One was listed at St. Peter in the 1930 census, but she was eighty-five years old, which presents some believability issues with regard to the poem. We would love to find something more conclusive.

In Jim Curran's 1937 account of his time at St. Peter, he used the pseudonym "Mrs. Harms" for the nurse matron as the chief disciplinarian. Perhaps, to disguise an off-color hospital staff, Martha also used pseudonyms?

If Mary was a patient, then the "prison garb" mentioned could have been a canvas or denim dress. The "gig" could be referencing a temporary or unofficial job. Sometimes, due to a lack of adequate staffing, hospital attendants were hired from within, or patients asked to help the staff. Patients may have been implicitly rewarded for assistance such as tackling and restraining others. By turning a blind eye to patient-on-patient violence, hospital staff could remain blameless.

An eerily similar story to "Mary" comes from Dr. William Hammond's asylum research, published in *The International Review*. He included details of a force-feeding episode witnessed at St. Peter State Hospital:

> "In the asylum at St. Peter, Minnesota, a patient who refused to eat had his mouth filled with food by a nurse, and the mess pushed down into his stomach with the handle of a knife, while another nurse held him down.
>
> On one occasion he ran away, yelling that they wanted to kill him. He was caught and laid on a bench; one attendant held his hands, and sat across his body; another attendant and a patient helped to hold him; his mouth was plugged to prevent his closing it. The food (soup) was poured in from a pitcher; his breath was heard to 'gurgle' as the soup went into his windpipe, and in five minutes he was dead."

(Source: Hammond, W. A. (1880). The Treatment of the Insane. *The International Review*, VII(March), pp. 225-241.)

42. "Fated Chase"

Upon a bucking bronco,
A rider, stern and bold,
Is riding o'er the mountains
On wint'ry night so cold.

The snow, like stars, is sparkling
Beneath the horse's feet.
He has no place of shelter,
Nor anything to eat.

A pack of hungry coyot's
Had followed in his track.
He lit a torch of safety
To keep those wild beasts back.

His bronco, all exhausted,
And would no longer pace.
The snow is heavy falling
To cover up his trace.

He escaped from a prison
Where he was held for crime.
He knew he was not guilty
And would not serve his time.

He crept deep in lion's den
And asked his Lord to save.
Now, a true-hearted man, he,
In that treacherous cave.

Cold and hungry, he grew weak,
And there, was forced to lie.
He knew that he'd not long exist –
That he would soon to die.

He begged the Lord to take his soul.
His hopes were to an end.
By unjust laws, left accused
To die without a friend.

V: While He And Dad

43. Forgotten.

To Louis and Ralph.

I'm gone and on forgotten
By one I can't forget.
The one I one time sheltered,
Before he drew a breath.

Beneath my heart, he slumbered.
He did not know of life.
With suffering, I bore him,
With pains of cutting knife.

Weak and helpless, I was left,
I never could get well.
Devil came, destroyed my life,
And changed it all to hell.

From then, I was forsaken,
By husband, child, and friend.
And put into a dungeon,
To suffer with no end.

Editorial Comments

Heavy speculation surrounds this poem and its correct interpretation. Theories on its meaning include stillbirth, abortion, cecesarian section, postpartum depression, and others. At this time, we are comfortable leaving the reader guessing.

In the 1982 book, *The Yellow Wallpaper* by Charlotte Perkins Stetson, a short story is included about a woman with postpartum depression (unofficially termed) in the 1800s. She describes her husband's decision to have her committed in isolation as an act of kindness and love. He believed keeping his wife removed from responsibility, could give her time to heal from her unexplainable nervous disorder. This example causes one to question if Louis Jr.'s participation in Martha's committal was, in a way, more sympathetic than cruel.

Hospital historian, Beth Zabel, has explained that in the 1920s, "rest and isolation from stress were the common treatment for nerves," and that the asylum did provide opportunities for this type of therapeutic stay (2021, October 22, Personal communication to Janelle Molony).

Illustration 31: September 20, 1926. "Ralph, 4 years, 10 mo. old. M. 36, L. 42." Martha and Ralph hold stems of Crested Cockscomb Celosia. Louis' shadow can be seen cast over Ralph's body.

Credit: Louis Nasch Jr. Courtesy of Ralph Nasch.

44. The Vacant Chair

To Louis and Ralph.

The vacant chair that has been left
sits idle in your home,
I will try to make a rhyme of it
and put it in a poem.

I will try to draw a scene of it—
a scene so odd and rare,
so you may picture memories
of someone in that chair...

Your home was always tidy.
You never found it mussed.
But now, I can imagine
it's covered up with dust.

But what is there to cleanliness
when souls are raven black,
and the devil's got me in his snare,
where I never come back.

[cont.]

That chair, long left behind me,

to you, I hope is dear,

so you and Ralph may cherish it,

as if a souvenir.

It's sitting in your dining room,

presented by a friend

who had a life, unpleasant,

and embittered, he did end.

Editorial Comments

The first stanza shows an awareness of Martha's own cleverness with words and a practice that she may be consciously trying to improve on. In later poems, she reiterates how she conveys her feelings through poetry and recommends this to a family member. Perhaps, she felt writing was therapeutic or healing.

The strange, final stanza relates to a note written into the margin of the page that reads, "Chair presented by C. Wiener." Louis Jr.'s cousin and neighbor from across the street, Charles Wiener Jr. (1892-1931), died by suicide at the age of thirty-nine. A family descendant believes this was due to depression and possibly related to financial worries.

45. Our Mamma.

To Louis and to Ralph.
Written from Ralph's point of view.

'Tis sad and silent everywhere. The voice we loved is stilled.
She left us with a vacant chair that never can be filled.

Our home is sad and lonely
When we enter it at night.
The sweetness of a Mamma
Is still missing from our sight.
Was our home just meant for two?
Just for me and just for you?
Must we struggle on through strife
As I live this vacant life?
Tell me, Daddy, will you tell
Why has Mamma gone to hell?
Was I born from one so mean
Who on earth could not be seen?

Why was her God so cruel to her, to let her go and stray?
Instead of helping her do right, he took her world away.

He led her right off into hell, away from you and me.
And there, to suffer forever, the world no more to see.

Editorial Comments

Martha has used the "voice" metaphor in other poems of eulogy form, though here, she uses it on herself, as if she were the one deceased (**See #69 "Sympathy" and #71 "A Mother Gone"**).

Originally written in six quatrains, this poem has been arranged to distinguish Marth's shift in meter. Stanzas one, three and four follow her signature 8-6 meter, while stanza two is a strict 7-syllable meter.

46. A Scene From Beyond.

To Louis and Ralph.

You see so many pretty scenes
Of brooks and trees and flowers,
Where you and Ralph may go to view
And spend your lonely hours.

And you sit beneath a shady tree,
Like baby days, when Ralph was small,
Where you then, both, can think of me
Like when we didn't know I'd fall.

God put his beauty everywhere
For human eyes to see,
For those he thinks to deserve it.
But not for one like me.

[cont.]

If I could draw an airplane
And also make it fly,
I'd put Ralph and you in it,
To soar right through the sky.

I'd give you both a chance to ride
And have you going free,
So you could come at any time
When you'd wish to see me.

Editorial Comments

The third stanza is echoed in "The Cross of Calvary," when Martha feels God has not forgiven her from any transgressions she might have committed.

The poetic structure is a medley of Martha's familiar meter schemes. By stanza: 8-7, 8-8, 8-6, 7-6, then 8-6 again. She maintains her signature aBcB rhyme scheme throughout all five quatrains.

VI: Frolic In Fun

47. No Where.

You're a million miles from no where,

        but few miles from

        your home.

To help loved ones know your feelings:

        send thoughts to them

        in poem.

48. Bows.

I'm sending you bows of ribbons for you to remember

me by. Select the one that you favor and wear it as a

collar tie:

If, of me, you sometimes think,

Wear my little bow of pink.

If your love for me is true,

Wear my little bow of blue.

And, if your love for me is dead,

Please send back my bow of red.

49. A Bed.

An Ode.

The thing you most do value,
Be it clothed blue or red,
When you're aching and tired:
Your flouncy, homelike bed.

At dawn, when you awaken,
You shake your drowsy head
And wish it were twilight, for
You have to leave your bed.

It assesses aches and pains.
In illness, it is gold.
It's the place to cuddle up
When winter nights are cold.

And when the world seems black, dull,
For life, you no more care,
Then kneel right at your bedside
And speak to God in Prayer.

Editorial Comments

The fact that Martha calls her bed at the hospital a hard board or bench in this poem does not necessarily indicate that she was simply sleeping on a bed that was not well-cushioned. The possibility that Martha was made to remain on an actual bench for extended periods does exist and should not be discounted.

A hospital historian has explained that mobile patients were made to "get up, get dressed, [and] make their beds early in the morning. They then moved to hallways or dayrooms which had long benches and sometimes, wooden chairs" (Zabel, B., 2021, October 22, Personal communication to Janelle Molony).

50. Rhyme.

If you could rhyme, as I have, which no one can deny,

You'd have some easy sailing to make your living by.

Editorial Comments

Martha is aware of the attention her poems receive. She appears to value her talent and knows she is improving.

51. Home Sweet Home.

Let it be your motto,

As on through life you roam—

There's no other place on earth,

To you, so dear, as home.

Stones and sand upon the land.

Wet rocks in deep, blue sea.

When you read these little rhymes, Dear,

Do try to think of me.

52. Birthday Rhymes.

A precious day

has come again!

You feel so proud you're still on Earth.

You do not know

how long you'll stand,

until you've had a second birth.

Your struggles and strife,

no longer known,

when *Paradize* is now your hearth.

Editorial Comments

The spiritual commentary includes a rebirth that she describes as her key to eternal life in heaven, though it may not be specifically referencing a traditional baptismal rebirth. In Lutheran traditions, a baptism is typically performed in one's infancy. Later, in a letter, Martha is described as being "6 ½" years old (**see Appendix**). The letter writer suggests a spiritual do-over that is above and beyond her formal religious practices. This may be connected to Christian Scientist ideas of the time.

Illustration 32: Ralph Nasch's confirmation at Old Emanuel Lutheran Church, Sunday, April 14, 1935.

Louis Jr. wrote about this day: "Ralph had a nice big white flower in his left button hole of his new suite [sic]. ... and a white handkerchief in your suit jacket. You looked very sharp Ralph" (1987).

Credit: Unknown photographer. Shared by Lori Sudgen via *Ancestry.com*.

53. A Graceful Story

Bring your heartaches,

    hide your tears,

    to save your youthful look.

Those drawn lines

    will show in years,

    like print inside a book.

Editorial Comments

These lines appear again in "Life in Northern Pines" in reference to being outwardly tough after disappointments.

54. "Mother's Day"

What a wonderful honor,

This day, given to you,

With flowers presented

In every light hue.

Be thankful you are a mother;

A mother so loyal and true.

To have the love of children

Which God has bestowed unto you.

The hand that rocks the cradle

Shall rule on sea and land,

To keep the world replenished

With human race so grand.

55. "Christmas Wishes"

The kind of Christmas I wish for you

Is one that is made of dreams come true.

One that will warm and thrill and bless,

One that will bring you happiness,

One that is holy, gay and glad,

The best kind of Christmas you've ever had.

56. Rhyme of Months.

JANUARY

Begin the year with ice and snow.

It is the month you most do fear when Northern Winds do blow.

FEBRUARY

Still, it is cold, but not so long.

The wind is rather fierce and bold, and blows on you so strong.

MARCH

Spring arrives, snow is *thaughing* fast.

This is the time you look ahead, when winter will soon pass.

APRIL

Small buds appear under bright sun.

In warmth, no more sorrow to fear. The honeybees soon come.

MAY

For you, the nicest month of all—

When songbirds come to make their nest, and for their mates, they call.

JUNE

In shade, you gather some flowers.

You long for the thundershowers to bring a cooling breeze. [cont.]

183

JULY

The hottest month, with cyclones feared.

When grain is ripe and corn is tall, the binders then appear.

AUGUST

The evening Whippoorwill, you hear.

Everything seems dry and half-dead as fall is drawing near.

SEPTEMBER

Heavy apples hang so mellow.

You hear the song of Mourning Doves and pumpkins will yellow.

OCTOBER

Frost strikes now. Leaves come flitting down.

Prepare yourself as winter nears, and nuts turn ripe and brown.

NOVEMBER

Off you go, sport hunting deer.

The days are cold and short. It's time the snow appears.

DECEMBER

Oh, Christmas, come. To Savior, sing.

To children, lots of cheer and sweets, and all joy, to them, bring.

Editorial Comments

In the July stanza, corn "binders" are tractor-driven carts that can roll, cut and pack the stalks to be tied into bundles. The repeated references to farm life (grain, corn, apples, pumpkins, nuts), and the reference to hunting deer in November give us reason to believe this poem was written either for or about the Gruening family farm near Henderson, Minnesota. At the time of Martha's writing, Only her mother Augusta, and brother Hugh live on the farm.

Originally presented in quatrain (48 lines), rearranged into 12 tercets, following an 8-8-6 meter.

VII: I Reflect On

57. The Gruenings.

Across the cold, foaming waters, where the sun shines at night, 'twas there my dear old Mütterchen first saw the rays of light. 'Twas there, she spent her life in youth and wished for love and fame—to find someone of her own choice, to change her maiden name.

On the days of sunshine weather, she and dad both strolled together, hand-in-hand, all the scenes to see, and sat beneath a shady tree. They did not care how long they sat. Their time was spent in lovers' chat. They did not know of want, nor fear. Their wedded life was drawing near.

In happiness, they soon did wed. Their future seem so wide when poverty stood at their door and comfort was denied.

They struggled on for many years. Their life was met with joy and tears. Eager in heart, and in their hands, they chose to see a better land. They came across deep seas of blue, ashore'd to place they never knew.

[cont.]

Then, one by one, their children came, till by them six babes bore their name. Dear, old dad did not come to stay. At fifty-three, he passed away. Then, one by one, they chose to roam and left their little country home. There was but one who stayed with Ma, to take up the place of his Pa. He did not care to have a wife—he chose to live a bachelor life.

Dear, old Mother is up in age and does not know of me—that I am penned into this cage, her never more to see.

Editorial Comments

If the final claim is true (that the family kept Martha's situation a secret from Augusta), this might indicate an immense level of shame, or sense of protection for the perceived frailness of Augusta Gruening's heart. The news might shock her and lead to an early death (per an old wives' tale). Martha's mother would have been age seventy-five in 1932.

Illustration 33: Circa 1919. Emma Gruening with new husband, Guy Ellsworth, a WWI Army transport driver.

After WWI, they moved to the Nasch neighborhood (**see Maps**). Guy became a taxi cab driver and coordinator. They never had children. By 1934, they divorced. Emma later moved back to the family farm near Henderson, MN, with her mother, Augusta, and brother, Hugh. She died of carcinoma cancer at the age of fifty-four.

Credit: Unknown photographer. Shared by Lori Sudgen via *Ancestry.com*.

Illustration 34: Circa 1941. Caption reads: "Grandma Gruening and Aunt Emma, a-way back when." Presumed to be taken at the family home near Henderson,

Minnesota. Augusta is approx. 84, and Emma, 43.

Credit: Possibly taken by Ralph Nasch. Courtesy of Ralph Nasch.

58. Loyalty and Love.

To You and Mother.

The one who is your dearest friend will come to you in need

She'll help you every way she can with kindness and with speed.

If mother is lonely and blue, and longs for a caress,

Pet her, as she once did for you, back in your cradle dress.

Editorial Comments

The "You" is Martha's sister Emma Gruening Ellsworth, and the mother is
Augusta Gruening, who is close to seventy-five at the time of Martha's writing.

Emma Gruening Ellsworth's marriage was under stress leading up to her divorce
from Guy Ellsworth in 1934. The exact reasons for their separation are unknown.
It is believed that, in difficult times, Emma retreated to the family home for relief,
just as her older sister Martha had done when Louis Jr. was suspected of cheating
(**also see "Life in Northern Pines"**). Guy remarried by the 1940s and started a
family with his second wife, while Emma never provided him children.

59. "Life in Northern Pines"

At morning dawn, when you awake, you toss
your drowsy head. You wish that it was midnight for
you dread to leave your bed. The house feels some cold
and clammy. The furnace must be low. You slip into a
housedress and to the kitchen you go.

Build a fire in the range to get the kitchen
warm. The household flies soon limber up, then they
began to swarm. Cook some mush and coffee, and fry
some eggs and meat. Then call to Hugh and Ma to
come inside to eat.

When you're through, you sit and think and plan
a fancy dish, then say to Fraú Gruening, "Let's go and
catch some fish." She is so spry and willing. She puts
on Hugh's old coat and off you go, fishermen, into a
rough built boat. Row out to the midst of lake. Some

[cont.]

pretty scenes you see, as autumn leaves are falling from

each and every tree.

After a long time waiting, the fish will not come

bite. You feel you're getting hungry with an upset

appetite! "Tomorrow," you say, "let's go home. There is

no use to try. We'll catch us a big, fat rooster and make

a tasty fry."

Slowly, you row back to the shore and feel that

you are beat. Just tell them *fuhy* fishes you'd rather eat

some meat! On your way home, meet Hugh with gun.

Along comes a rabbit. He shoots it while it's on the run.

You say, "Ma, we're in luck! We'll save that feathered

rooster's life, and roast up for dinner a white-tail

jackrabbit, tonight."

When you get back to the house, the postman

just gone by. So, go out to the mailbox, a letter there

from Guy. His message brings back memories of days

[cont.]

that have gone by. You longed so much to see him and

bitterly you cry, but bury your heartaches and hide your

tears to keep your youthful look, for those drawn lines

will show in years, like print within a book.

Do not pine and worry. Do not live in despair.

Put your trust in Jesus. He will answer your prayer.

Editorial Comments

The first stanza is a refrain from the poem #49 "A Bed." The penultimate stanza is a refrain from #53 "A Graceful Story."

The "You" in this poem is Emma Gruening Ellsworth (Martha's younger sister). "Fraü Gruening" is Martha's mother, Augusta Gruening. "Hugh" is Martha's older brother Hugo Gruening (1887-1967). Guy Ellsworth (1892-1955) was Emma Gruening's husband (Martha's brother-in-law).

60. Dearest Mother.

What can we do for you, Dear Mother,

to cheer you until end?

You do not ask a sole thing from us,

but be a loyal friend.

Editorial Comments

If what Matha said in her poem "The Gruenings" is true about her own mother, Augusta, not knowing about her commitment, then it can be assumed no direct communication occurred between them. Any poems or letters to her might have been routed through Louis Jr. or Emma, depending on the content.

61. Futures and *Advantures.*

To Brother.

There are trains for you to go on. There are ships for you at sea.
There are futures and *advantures,* but there is no world for me.

Do you think of our dear childhood that was thirty years ago,
when we stood by one another like two flowers in a row?

When we played in green pastures and we ran like little deer…
Now, you ask how am I feeling, and your eyes are filled with tears.

Human eyes that are about me, they are burdened by my sight.
They wish that I would vanish in the darkest time of night.

If there ever was a Jesus, he must have a heart of stone,
as to see this horrid suff'ring and forever hear me groan.

Some loving hands try to help me and they know not what to do.
Then, they go away disgusted. So does Louis, Ralph, and (now) you.

Editorial Comments

Martha has three brothers: Richard (1884-1921), Hugo ("Hugh" 1887-1967), and Leopold (1893-1934). Considering the known responsibilities of "Hugh" as a homemaker-bachelor and caretaker to their senior mother, the best guess for the brother she is addressing is Leo, who was friends with Louis and may have sided with him in the eventual separation.

Leo lost one leg above the knee early in his life due to tuberculosis and after receiving an artificial leg, he chose to enter the prosthetics industry as a leg maker. The cause of Leo's death in 1934 is documented as "got sick" in Louis Jr.'s records.

62. "Friendship"

Plenty of friends will smile with you

When you have sunshine everywhere,

When your clouds are white

And sky is blue,

Those pleasant friends will linger there.

But will those friends stick by your side

The day when you must call in need?

When the last ray of hope

Has withered and died,

Will they offer a helping deed?

I want friends who will stick and stay

When life seems like a fog at night

When darkness rolls in

And I can't find my way,

They cling to me with all their might.

63. A Friend.

Friend of my dream, how perfect you seem.

Your future is ever so wide.

There are hundreds of men, time and again,

That would offer to make you their bride.

Sometimes, I think you're a beautiful link

To fellows, who form like a chain,

To offer their love and coo like a dove,

In trying, your friendship, to gain.

You're pretty and neat. You're loving and sweet.

Your voice is tender and kind.

Wherever you roam, on land or on foam,

Companions, you always will find.

Some time in June, by the light of the moon,

When lovers hold hands and sigh,

You'll make a little nest for the one you love best,

And let the rest of the world go by.

64. Dearest Friend.

To Mrs. Krumm.

The closest friend I ever had,

The only one I knew,

Was Mrs. Krumm, my dearest friend.

She was so kind and true.

Her face was always sunshine.

Her heart was full of love.

She was just like an angel

Who has a home above.

She'd greet me in the morning.

Her voice was calm and sweet.

There never was another

With her, who would compete.

She tried so hard to help me

When I was down and out.

She tried to lift that heavy block

That blocked a sinner's mouth.

Her tender hands were powerless.

Her heart felt like a rock

When she knew that she was helpless

And could not lift that block.

I shall wish her health and wealth

And everything in store.

I shall wish her peace and pleasures

And happiness galore.

Editorial Comments

This poem includes an important and unusual detail regarding a "sinner's mouth" being somehow blocked. In the Epilogue, we will revisit this as a significant clue to answering what may have caused Martha to have been committed in the first place.

Illustration 35: December 18, 1944. Guests at Ralph Nasch's wedding. (Left to right) Mrs. Anna M. Krumm (1876-1947), her grandson, Jerry Klinger, Jerry's mother, Miss Dorothy Krumm ((1919-1999, **also see illustration 11**), and Ralph Nasch. Per a family historian's records, Jerry found Louis Jr. dead in the yard, in 1964.

1st Lieut. Ralph Louis Nasch returned to the United States from Europe after flying a remarkable twenty-five bomber missions with the U.S. Army Air Force during World War II. His last mission was in February of 1944. He returned home in April, promptly proposed to his highschool sweetheart, Marie Lancette, at Cherokee Park in St. Paul, then married her on December 18, at the St. Louis Catholic Chapel in downtown St. Paul.

Credit: Unknown photographer. Courtesy Ralph Nasch.

65. An Old Fashion Dwelling.

Written for Anna Paape.

An old fashion dwelling, sitting up high:

Its shingles are withered, its sidings are dry.

You honor and cherish this dear, ancient home.

It belonged to your mother when on earth she did roam.

She lived in this dwelling for many long years.

Her life was complete with joy and with tears.

This wonderful mother, through struggles and strifes

Gave to her children, their beautiful *lifes*.

This home, to you, is valued as if gold.

The thoughts of your childhood bring memories of old.

A modern mansion, so lovely in grace

Could not compare with this old fashion place.

Editorial Comments

When Anna Weiner married Arthur Paape, she moved into a home with him, just two doors down from her mother's original St. Paul home (**see Maps**). In 1926, Anna's mother, Theresa Doerrler Weiner, died in in her mid-60s (**see Family Trees**).

Illustration 36: Anna Rosalia Paape (née Wiener, 1900-1983), undated. Anna is Louis Jr's first cousin and daughter of Charles and Theresa Wiener, who all lived across the street from the Nasches, on Hall Avenue (**see Maps**).

Credit: Unknown photographer. Courtesy of Ralph Nasch.

Illustration 37: Arthur W. Paape (left, 1922-1998) with Ralph Nasch (right) at Como Park, circa 1926-27. . Ralph's cousin "Art," is the only child of Arthur and Anna Paape.

Credit: Unknown photographer. Courtesy of Ralph Nasch.

204

66. A Bride.

A precious day you hold dear
Has come to you in this year;
A day you'll honor all your life,
That you became a happy wife.

Let your face be always sunshine.
Let your smile be always sweet.
Let your arms be ever embracing,
When with hubby, Dear, you meet.

Since you've started life together,
Be a most loyal friend.
You will meet with stormy weather,
But be patient to the end.

Clouds will move and drift away,
Sun, again, be shining.
Love, alone, will lead the way
To see the silver lining.

Do your share and duties.
Do not shirk a one.
You will be rewarded
When all your tasks are done.

Editorial Comments

One person in the Nasches social circle who married between 1928-1932 was
Louis Jr.'s step-brother Henry Englebert Nasch. He married Esther Rose Yaeger
approximately 1928. Martha would have missed the wedding.

If, however, the bride in reference was not a family member, it could be about a
personal friend, or even, as seen in other poems, about a fellow patient at the
hospital.

In "Courtship Days," Martha elaborates on the stormy weather expression. In this
third stanza, she offers wisdom (warnings) based on her own experience.

This five quatrain poem combines both AABB and aBcB rhyme schemes and a
mixed 6, 7, 8 meter that is inconsistent. The tone is quite casual, not matching
Martha's usual standard or attention to detail.

67. A Shop Girl.

Written for Agnes Meyer, by request.

Every day, she goes to work
On feet so neat and small.
You'd think she were a wee miss
Of only two years tall.

She goes along with a skip.
Only eight blocks to walk
To a little baker shop.
About the cakes, she talks.

She sells the fancy doughnuts
And all kinds of warm pie,
Butter rolls and coffee cake,
White bread and marbled rye.

It makes a fellow hungry
To see her smiling face
From back behind the counter,
With sweet goods on a plate.

The thing she most does enjoy,
She can't deny by heck:
Every time, when payday comes,
To get a nice, big check.

In evening, when her work is done,
She goes back to her home.
She finds a letter waiting
In it, this little poem.

Editorial Comments

Based on family photographs, Agnes Meyers was not necessarily a short person. The "wee miss" comment could be in reference to the child-like skipping activity. We have not yet identified a bakery that is within eight blocks of the neighborhood, in any direction.

Illustration 38: The Meyers family, circa 1919. They lived around the corner from the Nasches in the 1930s, at 15 Augusta St. (**see Maps**). Back row (left to right): Mrs. Cecelia Sieben Meyers, Miss Agnes Meyers (born 1901), Lydia, Elenore, Loretta. Middle row: Willian, Frances, Anthony, George. Front row: Delores.

Credit: Unknown photographer. Originally shared by Katie Paulson on *Ancestry.com*.

VIII: People I've Lost

68. "Mother's Flowers"

In a beautiful garden of flowers

Dipped in a summer morning dew,

Out strolls dear, little grey-haired Mütter,

Those beautiful flowers to view.

Flowers are always at her hand

From Springtime until Fall.

She will care for them and cherish them,

She loves them, one and all:

With Morning Glories twining

And Asters, big and small,

Verbenas creeping o'er the ground

And Hollyhocks so tall.

With Four O'Clocks that bloom at eve

And spread their fragrance wide,

And Poppies growing here and there

And pretty Morning Bride.

[cont.]

With Pansies and Petunias

And Moss Roses, red,

All arranged with greatest care,

And formed into a bed.

With Marigold and Cockscomb

And Phlox of every hue,

With Sweet Peas and Nasturtiums

And Larkspur, pink and blue.

With Zinnias and Dahlias

And Gladiolas, tolle,

With Snapdragons and with Cosmos

Which bloom so late in fall.

With Carnations and with Tulips

And Balsam, white and pink,

With Peonies and with Iris

(I have named them well, I think).

[cont.]

With Roses and Forget-Me-Nots

And Honeysuckle sweet,

With Bleeding Heart and Fire Beams,

Now makes her lot complete.

She gathers them in large bouquet

When friends come by to see,

And offers them with greatest joy.

Her heart is filled with glee.

Her house plants are her winter joy

Of species odd and rare,

Each day she'll place them in the sun

And water them with care.

Their wonderful, little Mütter,

So prudent and so brave,

Shall have her last wish granted

With flowers upon her grave.

Editorial Comments

Louis Nasch maintained a lush garden at their cottage home, presumably started by his grandmother, Mary Kahles. Per family recollections, his flowers (especially the Celosia Cockscomb), were a particular stunner and he was known to bunch them to sell in bouquets to the neighborhood.

Illustration 39:
August, 1928. "Ralph, 6 years, 9 mo. old. Ralph in front of the flocks [Phlox] and a cockscomb flower in front of him. He is smiling. L. 44, M. 38."

This image is one of very few that survived from the span of 1928-1934. Ralph has noted in his scrapbooks how unusual it is that his childhood images from the time of Martha's committal disappeared from the family's collection. Both he and his father enjoyed taking photographs.

Credit: Louis Nasch Jr. Courtesy of Ralph Nasch.

69. Sympathy.

Written for Henry in Time of Death. 1932.

Dearest Friend, I am so sorry

That you're saddened by such grief.

If I only could do something

To give comfort and relief.

If your heart is overladen

And you feel that you are lost,

Try to find a hope in Jesus.

He will lift that heavy cross.

Do not weep and do not worry,

Do not pine your life away.

As you know, and know it truly,

That you are not here to stay.

[cont.]

You will meet her and will greet her

When your earthly strife is o'er.

You will row that boat to safety

And will anchor at her shore.

Yes, I know how you do miss her,

For to see her smile once more.

And I know how you are longing,

For her to be at your door.

Oh, how hard it is to enter

In a home so dark and still.

Dearest Friend, do not murmur, as

You know it was God's will.

She's gone, but not forgotten

By you, with eyes so wet.

The sound of her loving voice,

You won't and can't forget.

[cont.]

She did her share and duties.

She *tryed* her *verry* best.

The one who now has claimed her

Will grant eternal rest.

Editorial Comments

There is an 1894 Spaulding and Grey song titled, "When You Know The Girl You Love Loves You," where the expression "You will meet her and greet her with a kiss," may have influenced Martha's writing.

Louis Nasch Jr. had a younger step-brother named Henry Englebert Nasch (1889-1981). Henry was a waggoner (transport driver) in the U.S. Army during World War I. Military records and family genealogical records show Henry married an Esther Rose Yaeger (1892-1973) in either 1927 or 1928. Their child, Dorcas Nasch, was a lifelong friend and pen pal of Ralph Nasch.

A January 12, 1932 obituary of an Ester Mathilda Rowe (1896-1932), aged 36, who is described as the beloved wife of Henry Nasch. Louis Nasch Jr. transcribed the details of this obituary in his family records and may have delivered the news to Martha at one of his visits.

70. In Memory.

My darling, dear, it's lonely here,
Since you have gone away.
Our tender care, our love and prayer
Could never make you stay.

Like a little flower, you grew.
You were our joy and pride.
When illness came into our home,
It took you from our side.

Now, our hearts are filled with grief
And our home is still.
We will try to find relief,
As it was God's will.

In memory, a stone we'll carve
And place it at your head.
A verse or two to rhyme so true,
Of tears that we have shed.

All your little toys, we will save,
And every thing in store,
Until the roll for us is called
To meet you on that shore.

Editorial Comments

The "God's will" phrase creates an association to the poem, "Sympathy," perhaps indicating the two deceased females were a mother and her child. If there is a death-by-childbirth, it might have been recorded as "puerperal fever." Also, regarding a grave and headstone, if there is a mother-child connection, then the two would likely have been buried together in the same grave.

71. A Mother Gone.

'Tis sad and silent everywhere.
The voice we loved is gone.
She left us with an empty chair
To enter home beyond.

She once was our darling mother.
Her love was true and dear.
The tender sweetness of her voice
We loved and longed to hear.

She was our pal in cradle days,
She bore each burden well.
She was patient in all her ways,
Our lips will kindly tell.

She done her share and duties—
She did not shirk a one.
The one who now has claimed her
Pronounced her work, "Well done."

72. Mother's Ways.

Was ever a pal like mother? Or was ever one so true?
There never could be another; a pal that was like you.

In illness, it was our belief that you could soothe and heal.
We always felt such great relief when you would, by us, kneel.

You *tryed* so hard to help us to chose the smartest path.
You shared your recipe for how to avoid sin's dark wrath.

You taught me right from wrong way. You taught me how to pray.
You showed us short from the long way, so we might not go astray.

At night, you knelt beside us. We felt your presence near.
Through darkness, you would guide us. We had no one to fear.

And if we follow in your track, regret will not be known.
It must lead to a place on high, where *Paridize* is shown.

IX: Faith, Undone

73. The World.

The world is filled with wonders and put on earth to stay.

The lakes, the cliffs and desert will never pass away.

The hail, the rain and sunshine will ever come and go.

The summer with its foliage, and winter covered snow.

The wave upon the ocean, the shark in depths of sea,

Have come to stay forever and scenes will always be.

The beast within the forest, the hawk upon the wing,

The lambkin in the meadow and birds will always sing.

There always will be countries, races, color and creed.

Those make up a perfect world, and war in time of need.

There always will be pleasure and always will be strife

As such is God's creation within the human life.

Editorial Comments

Originally presented in eight rhyming quatrains, but combined into couplets to ease reading. Curiously, this condensing of the poem's length revealed a perfect thirteen syllable meter in each (combined) line of the new couplets. The number is suspicious and it is difficult to determine if this was an intentional structure. Besides being an unlucky number in many superstitions, the astrological significance is one of suffering and death.

74. Flowers.

Wildflowers are so pretty!
They need no care from hand.
They thrive and bloom most everywhere,
O'er hillside and on land.

They grow in fields and forest fair,
On broken sod and plain.
They spread their beauty here and there,
In sunshine and in rain.

You may gather them in Springtime,
You may gather them in Fall.
Their fragrance is so pleasing.
They grow for one and all.

Their little seeds each year are sown
By nature's mighty pow'r,
For all to see them grow and bud
And burst into a flow'r.

[cont.]

Garden flowers are precious, too,
Like jewels among the lot.
You care for them and cherish them
Until they're nipped by frost.

At season time, you transplant them
And place them in a row.
And there they stand, 'till seeds are ripe,
Then covered up by snow.

Flowers are part of memories:
They are carried by bride,
Fragrance, color, cherished by all,
Loved with fondness and pride.

75. Disappointment.

Disappointment is part of life,
But it does not help to frown.
You might as well keep on smiling,
Then to let grief break you down.

Cheer up and keep on with smiling
When others sparkle bright with fun.
And keep it up, and don't forget
That smiles help each and every one.

No one can save you from sorrows.
And when you frown, they'll disappear.
Try to smile away heartaches,
At least, pretend you're full of cheer.

When shadows darken your sky,
And everything seems wrong,
Take a breath, seek God for strength,
And clouds will move along.

76. Untitled.

How sweet and tasteful the hours,

When you've hope in Jesus to see.

Sweet birds, sweet bees, and sweet flowers

Are bountifully heaped upon thee.

Editorial Comments

A dashed line and note separated this poem from "Disappointment." The note reads: "This verse does not belong to the other four." Thi, single quatrain is a positively rephrased refrain from, "Suffering."

77. Lake Pleasures.

7	On the lake, you wish to go
7	For to fish or pleasant row
7	In a boat so big and wide,
7	With some loved one at your side.
8	But stop to think—you're not on land,
8	That drowning may be close at hand.
8	You may go out so well and sound
8	And may capsize and go right down.
9	There is a Reaper whose name is death,
6	And with his sickle keen,
9	He will reap the bearded grain at breath,
6	And flowers grown between.
9	But those who do not fear the knife
6	Are better off, dear friend,
9	As there is no way to save your life
6	When life is to an end.

8	Do just as nature tells you to
6	When on the sea or land.
8	Your life was chose before your birth,
6	How long that you may stand
8	Your life is much like a flower:
6	It needs the sun and rain.
8	And when you are matured in age,
6	You're reaped like golden grain.

Editorial Comments

Meter marks have been added intentionally.

Stanzas two and three echo a Henry Wadsworth Longfellow poem, "The Reaper and the Flowers," from *Voices in the Night*, and published in The World's Best Poetry anthology, volume III, in 1904. The original poem speaks of a mother (possibly Mother Earth) having to surrender her flowers (metaphorical children) to the Reaper and Angel of Death. She must do so not in cruelty or because of God's wrath, but because the Lord had need of the flowers in Paradise, and that they were being transplanted into God's own garden.

Martha's lines, "Your life is much like a flower: It needs the sun and rain," promote the ideas for sustaining life through the light and energy of the Creator, and surrendering one's food as a form of self-sustenance.

78. "Nature's Beauty"

To the world of nature's beauty,

Songbirds flying to and fro'—

Artists sketching pretty scenes

Of mountains topped with brilliant snow,

Babbling brooks reflecting sun,

Those twilight rays of gold,

Evening chimes of Angelica

Bring memories of old.

Waterfalls and morning dew,

Turtle Doves who build and coo,

Butterflies and humming bees,

Grapevines climbing into trees.

In the meadows, lambkins bleat,

Daisies twining o'er their feet,

Flowers spread o'er hills and *plaine,*

Fields filled in with golden grain.

Drifting clouds are sailing by

Rainbow colors in the sky.

Autumn leaves, copper and red,

Over fields and mountains spread.

Chestnuts from trees are falling.

Whippoorwill, Bobwhite calling.

Stars are falling here and there.

Snowflakes, whirling in the air.

For everything there is place

For nature's beauty and grace.

Editorial Comments

The chimes of Angelica references a tin, non-motorized musical decoration used at the Christmas season, otherwise called Angel Chimes. These German-originated Glockenspiel are operated by the heat from candle flames rising to spin a small turbine fan above. When the fan turns, the dangling, decorative hammers activate bells. In some references, the traditional expression for this is, "As candles burn, Angels turn."

79. "Thankful"

Be thankful that you're not like me,
That you're a child of God.
The beauties of the world, you see,
As on thru life, you *throad*.

May creed and friendship always be.
Dishonor, be outcast.
May loyalty be heaped on thee,
And cling to you so fast.

Be thankful for the light of world.
Be thankful for your health.
The life that God has given you
Is worth far more than wealth.

Be thankful for your rest and sleep,
Which is bestowed on you,
When peaceful dreams upon you creep,
And make you feel like new.

[cont.]

Be thankful that you walk upright.
You fear no one to face.
God knew when he created you
To give you that good grace.

Be thankful you have a shelter,
Even though it's a loan.
Be it ever small and humble,
It is a place called "home."

Be thankful that you are not lost,
That in God's hands you dwell.
For here I am, lost forever,
Suff'ring alive in hell.

80. "The Cross of Calvary"

Upon a mountain called Calvary, there stood a rugged cross.

I now must bear that cross on me, forever to be lost.

I must bear it in all the suffering and agony I find.

That rough and heavy weight on me, unknown to any mankind.

I hear so many tales of life and ongoing beauties of the world,

But what are all those but tales and lies, when from God's Earth I've

been hurled.

Beauty is nothing when still bearing my cross, as Christ has arisen,

But he did not come and rise for people like me, only for every other

race and nation.

Dying for their sins, he set them free,

But how could he be so unfaithful, as not to die and rise for me!

Even Christ died upon a heavy cross before the day was done.

And God looked on and saw his plight, though would not help his Son.

How much less would He do for one like me?

[cont.]

Beneath a boulder, I am firmly clasped by Satan and his snare.

Rocks of sin, piled high on my soul, forever to be kept there.

I cannot even call for the help of God, I've lost my future and hopes.

Forever in this hell, I must *throad,* where darkness claims me as a thief

in ropes.

He even stole away what I possessed:

My mate first, then the child I loved best.

Loved ones, pining, they come and go.

My unknown suff'ring, they cannot trace.

A salty trail now winds to and fro from sobs and tears upon my face.

End.

Editorial Comments

The "End" finish line adds clarity regarding the original order of poems, as curated by Martha and gently modified in this collection.

Ridiculed Across The Nation

(Epilogue)

How Media Mockery Cleared Martha's Name

Janelle Molony, M.S.L.

& Jodi Nasch Decker, Ed.D

Ridiculed Across The Nation

One month after Martha Nasch was released from St. Peter State Hospital for the Insane, her (then) husband, Louis Nasch Jr. contacted the press, declaring that Martha was still troubled with not sleeping, eating, and drinking, even after being under continuous medical care from June of 1927 until July of 1934. Louis Jr. stated his reason for going public with this news as, "I do not want people to think I am starving my wife" (Sioux City Journal, 1934, Sept. 19). It is unknown whether there ever was any rumors or allegations that Louis Jr. was doing such a thing, but appearing to be a negligent or abusive spouse would make him look bad, and make it easier for Martha to obtain a divorce, if she wanted one (**see "The Ballad of Martha"**).

In their September 18, 1934 press interview, Martha boldly stated that "the world will not believe me" when she described her medical condition and the symptoms, including feeling no need to eat (*Sioux City,* 1934). Louis Jr. made it clear he did not believe her at first, either, until he'd tried to catch her eating by surprise, "but I never could," he surmised (*South Bend Tribune*, 1934, Sept. 20).

From a Newspapers.com archival search and review of published articles resulting from this interview, we have been able to conclude there were six different versions of the story that circulated in a staggering total of ninety articles nationwide. From September 19 until November 3, 1934, Martha's story appeared in newspapers across the United States, twice in Canada, as well as receiving a mention in the weekly *Time* magazine.

Woman Has Gone Without Food, Drink 7 Years

St. Paul.—P—A 44-year-old St. Paul housewife, Mrs. Martha Nasch, who "knows the world will not believe me," asserted Tuesday that she has taken neither food nor drink for seven years.

Her husband, Louis J. Nasch, 55, a painter, who said he had not seen her eat or drink since July 29, said he had notified newspaper men of his wife's condition because "I do not want people to think that I am starving my wife."

Their 12-year-old son, Robert, who completes the household in which Mrs. Nasch does the cooking and other housework, added that his parents had "been telling everyone that my mom doesn't eat or drink anything."

Although unable to explain what she describes as "my supernatural condition," Mrs. Nasch expressed willingness to undergo tests to prove her claims.

"Place me under constant watch for any length of time," she said, "and I can prove that I do not need food or water."

When she first observed the change, Mrs. Nasch said, she consulted a physician and was confined, as a result, to a hospital for the insane for a time.

"My body felt and still feels," she declared "as though it were petrified. I feel well physically and my appearance has not changed since 1927."

Food, she added, is not repulsive, but her desire for it is gone.

When the seven-year fast began Mrs. Nasch weighed 140 pounds. Now she weighs 103.

Illustration 40: Sept. 19, 1934, *Sioux City Journal*, Iowa.

Credit: Associated Press. Accessed through Newspapers.com.

Woman Claims She Has Gone Seven Years Without Food

ST. PAUL, Minn., Sept. 20.— Although doctors scoffed at her story, Mrs. Martha Nasch, aged 44, a housewife, today contended that for seven years she has not eaten, nor drunk, nor slept.

Louis J. Nasch, 50, her husband, said:

"I've never seen her eat or drink. That's all I know. I've tried surprises to find her eating, but never have."

Mrs. Nasch interposed:

"I will submit to any test that may be asked if necessary. I will consent to an indefinite constant watch."

Nasch was one of three witnesses to sign Mrs. Nasch's statement concerning her condition. The others are Ralph Nasch, 12, their son, a high school student, and Lynette Claus, 18, a neighbor.

Mr. Nasch told reporters:

"I do not sleep, either. At least not like other people. I seem, rather, to be in a trance like someone under dental gas. It gives me no rest."

A St. Paul doctor who once had taken care of Mrs. Nasch said:

"I think it's all bunk!"

When your maid quits use a Tribune ad and get another.—Adv.

Illustration 41: Sept. 20, 1934, *South Bend Tribune,* Indiana.

Credit: Associated Press. Accessed through Newspapers.com.

The interview may have afforded Martha an opportunity to be validated and restored within her community. We don't know how many family members and neighbors were aware of her true reasons for hospitalization or the severity of her case, but this may have been an attempt to tell her story in a once-and-for-all manner. The only direct hints Martha leaves the reader are in two poems: In "The Gruenings," she implies that her own mother was kept unaware of the situation, and in "Dearest Friend," she implies her close friend Mrs. Krumm "tried to lift that heavy block that blocked a sinner's mouth."

Curiously, the story never ran in the St. Paul papers where it might have been originally intended to appear. If so, it might have quelled any nosy or judgemental neighbors who had learned of Martha's absence and teased her son, Ralph, to his childhood embarrassment. In "Outcast," she wrote pointedly that "The neighbors all shunned me and sneered in my face," prior to her asylum stay, though we cannot say for certain if it was immediately linked to her persistent complaints.

Martha's story quickly reached the Associated Press media center, the Newspaper Enterprise Association (N.E.A.), Chicago Tribune Publications, and eventually ACME. ACME then resold a blurb and a photo to their network members who needed something ready-made to spice up their next edition (see illustration 42). The blurb is dated September 19, 1934 and the N.E.A. catalog entry date shows September 22. Considering the original date of the Nasch interview (September 18), this shows a remarkably fast turn-around time for word to spread.

The back of the 8" x 6" black and white photo press release reads:

> *Mrs. Martha Nasch of St. Paul, Minn, shown above with her husband Louis J. Nasch, claims that she has not had any sleep, drank or eaten any food for a period of seven years. Although doctors of St. Paul scoof [sic] at the story, Mr. Nasch, a son, and a neighbor girl have signed a statement confirming the woman's claim. Mrs. Nasch says that she will submit to a test to back up her story.*

While some publications received the longer interview, most only saw the condensed ACME version. From there, each paper put their own spin on the story.

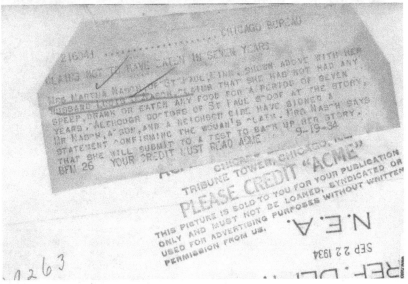

Illustration 42: Sept. 18, 1934. Louis J. Nasch Jr. (50) and Martha H. Nasch (44) pose outside their St. Paul, Minnesota home for a news media interview with an interviewer from the Associated Press and photographer from ACME.

Credit: N.E.A./ACME. Courtesy of Janelle Molony, owner of an original press release.

Martha's story ran under eleven different article titles. Over time, the editorial tone became increasingly mocking. The first several read:

- "Woman Has Gone Without Food, Drink 7 Years"
- "St. Paul Woman Claims She Hasn't Eaten, Drunk Anything for 7 Years"
- "No Food in 7 Years, Lives to Tell Story"
- "7-Years Faster And Husband"
- "Woman Says She Has Gone Seven Years Without Food"
- "Her 'Seven-Year Fast' is Derided"

Her 'Seven-Year Fast' Is Derided

Throw away your diet lists, girls, and take a lesson from Mrs. Martha Nasch, above, of St. Paul, Minn. Mrs. Nasch insists she has gone without food, without drink and without sleep for the last seven years, and feels fine at that. Of course, you may laugh, as do the doctors, but Mrs. Nasch, a son and a neighbor girl confirm her claim.

Illustration 43: "Her 'Seven-Year Fast'..." Sept. 25, 1934, *Latrobe Bulletin*, Pennsylvania.

Credit: ACME. Accessed through Newspapers.com.

Like in the children's whispering game, "Telephone," where a message is passed from one person to another by whispers, and minor interpretive errors perpetuate into major ones by the end, the stories about Martha Nasch became more erroneous over time. The following new copy was posted below her photograph in both the *Johnson City Press* (1934, Sept. 24) and the *Muncie Evening Press* (1934, Sept. 25):

Her 'Seven-Year Fast' is Derided
Throw away your diet lists, girls, and take a lesson from Mrs. Martha Nasch above, of St. Paul, Minn. Mrs. Nasch insists she has gone without food, without drink and without sleep for the last seven years, and feels fine at that. Of course, you may laugh, as do the doctors, but Mrs. Nasch, a son and a neighbor girl confirm her claim.

Another twist on this short scoop shows up in the October 1, 1934 *Fort Worth Star*, which reads:

Mrs. Martha Nasch, 44, St. Paul, Minn. Housewife, who says she has neither eaten, drunk nor slept in the past seven years, is shown with her husband, Louis, J. Nasch. Nasch 'verifies' his wife's claims. Nasch says that his wife's general health has not been harmed, and believes that she will live many years.

There is no inclusion of the last statement in this article from the press releases that ACME distributed (**see illustration 42**). Similarly, the dieting comment from other articles resources of more unsupported yellow journalism. As the story continued to be told and retold, it became absurd. The most laughable alteration in this series appears in the *Latrobe Bulletin* on September 25, 1934, where Martha's original thin-lipped mouth is replaced with a set of oversized teeth in an antiquated version of Photoshopping (**see illustration 44**). At this point, if Martha Nasch didn't already *sound* like a nutcase by the biased reporting, she surely appeared to *be* one from the composite image.

Then, *Time* magazine's October 8, 1934 edition featured a twenty-three word summary of Martha's plight with, "In St. Paul, Mrs. Martha Nasch swore that for seven years, she had not eaten a mouthful, drunk a drop, slept a wink." As shown, in less than sixty days, Martha's story of survival, healing, perseverance, and medical discovery was reduced to a punchline.

Illustration 44: 'Fasts Seven Years" Oct. 24, 1934, *Public Opinion*, Pennsylvania.

Credit: ACME. Accessed through Newspapers.com.

Fasts Seven Years

Mrs. Martha Nasch

Claiming she has not slept or partaken of any food or water for seven years, Mrs. Martha Nasch, above, 44, of St. Paul, Minn., offered to prove her feat to anyone or undergo any tests. Her husband declared he has never seen her eat, and is one of the three witnesses who signed a statement affirming Mrs. Nasch's declaration.

Illustration 45: Oct. 8, 1934 *Time* weekly magazine (cover).

Credit: ACME.

The Best Quotes Get Printed

Evident in the longer editorials that were printed, Martha seemed a willing accomplice to the media attention her husband invited, and she consented to disclosing her personal medical information. As quoted in the articles, Martha appeared to be self-aware and articulate. If we take a close look at some of her direct quotes (those without additional commentary or paraphrasing), we can hear her dare the reporter:

> "Place me under constant watch for any length of time and I can prove that I do not need food or water" (*Sioux City*, 1934, Sept. 19).

> "I will submit to any test that may be asked if necessary. I will consent to an indefinite constant watch" (*South Bend Tribune*, 1934, Sept. 20).

> "Let the test run six months if necessary" (*La Crosse Tribune*, 1934, Sept. 20).

Unfortunately, these incredulous claims do nothing but add to the impression that Martha is either delusional or lying her situation. There should be some allowance, however, for interpreting her words based on what *she* considered to be normal eating, drinking and sleeping. A well known way people can fast (abstain from or reduce food intake) is through a liquid-only diet. In many spiritual contexts (ignoring caloric intake), a liquid-only diet is considered a full abstinence from food and "eating" in the traditional sense (**see Introduction and notes on Breatharianism**). What if Martha was thoroughly convinced that her liquid meals in the hospital, such as those force-fed through a tube, did not count as "eating?" In any case, she shows a determination to have her chronic condition widely recognized and practically taunts the doctors at the State Hospital for being unable to find an answer.

If we consider for a moment that Martha knowingly exaggerated her story for the press, we are forced to also consider a most difficult act of deception. Could Martha have invented, played out, and perpetrated a seven-year-long hoax to dupe not only her husband, but also to confound doctors and baffle the public? To what end would she be trying to accomplish through such a feat? While we don't have a ready answer for that, we do know that maintaining an elaborate lie while under hospital supervision radically implausible compared to another alternative: Martha Nasch truly suffered from a very real, but then-misunderstood medical condition.

As a way to provide additional support for her claims, Martha asked for eyewitnesses to sign a written statement that attested to them never seeing her consume food or drink since she had returned home on parole, July 29, 1934 (see illustration 40). Those who allegedly participated were husband Louis Jr., son Ralph, and the next door neighbor Lynette Claus (see illustrations 47 & 48). Later articles liberally extended the period of eyewitness time to all seven years. Considering this date range includes when Martha lived away from the home, it's impossible to withstand any sort of scrutiny and we must disregard that revision.

Ralph Nasch would have been exactly twelve at the time of his mother's release. In discussions about her homecoming, he stated he had no memory of signing such a document.

Ralph Nasch has suggested the document Martha referred to in the *La Crosse Tribune* was just as fictitious as all her other claims, however, when asked again if he'd ever seen her eat or drink back then, he was stumped. With an embarrassed laugh, he answered with a firm, "no."

Another curiosity is that in the initial version of the article from *Sioux City*, Ralph is quoted as saying that Martha and Louis Jr. "had been telling everyone that my mom doesn't eat or drink anything," (1934, Sept. 19). Later, the *La Crosse Tribune* modified that quote to appear that Ralph was the one spreading the tales (1934, Sept. 20). To this alteration, we can definitively argue that Ralph was not spreading the news. For one, we know Ralph was

St. Paul Woman Claims She Hasn't Eaten, Drunk Anything For 7 Years

ST. PAUL, Minn.—A 44-year-old, bob-haired St. Paul housewife, who "knows the world will not believe me," averred today she has taken neither food nor drink for seven years.

Strong enough to cook and do the housework for her husband and son, Mrs. Martha Nasch sat mending socks in the front room of her little home at 642 Hall avenue as she stolidly maintained, under questioning of a reporter, that she has not eaten or drunk since 1927.

Across the room sat her husband, Louis J. Nasch, 55-year-old department store painter, who says he has not seen his wife eat or drink since July 29. The husband notified newspaper men of his wife's condition because "I do not want people to think I am starving my wife."

Twelve-year-old Robert Nasch, a student in Theodore Roosevelt junior high school, has, his parents said, smiling, "been telling every one that my mom doesn't eat or drink anything."

Although unable to explain completely what she describes as "my supernatural condition," Mrs. Nasch is willing to undergo a test under constant survelliance to prove her fasting claims.

"Place me under constant watch for any length of time," she said, "and I can prove that I do not need food or water. Let the test run six months if necessary."

Mrs. Nasch contends that when she first observed a change in her life she consulted a St. Paul physician. The result was confinement in the State Insane hospital at St. Peter.

"Somehow the world was not the same," she said. "My body felt and still feels as though it were petrified. I could not eat or drink. I did not want it, although I continued to get meals for my family.

"The doctor told me I had a case of nerves," she continued, "and because I refused to eat I was sent to St. Peter. There they tried to force feed me. They thought I was insane yet they told me I was normal in every other way. I read books, wrote and drew pictures. I hid or threw away the food brought me."

While in the hospital Mrs. Nasch sought through scientific books available to find some explanation of her condition.

"I found a plausible explanation in the Bible," she maintained, "although I never had paid much attention to the Bible up to that time. In the Old Testament I found this: 'They shall see food, but not eat. It shall be of wormwood. They shall see water, but not drink. It shall be as gall.' That describes perfectly my condition, but I cannot understand why this curse should be visited on me."

Illustration 46: Sept. 20, 1934, *La Crosse Tribune,* Wisconsin.

Credit: Associated Press. Accessed through Newspapers.com.

Illustration 47: June 2, 1929. Ralph Nasch with the next-door neighbor kids. (Left to right) Lynette Claus (b. 1918), Ralph, Genevieve Claus (b. 1920), and Dorothy Krumm (b. 1919). The Claus children lived at 636 Hall Ave. with their parents, Joseph G. Claus and Edna J. Kerr Claus. Lynette was interviewed in 1934 about Martha's eating habits. The Krumms lived around the corner from the Nasches on Augusta (present-day Baker Street).

Credit: Louis J. Nasch Jr. Courtesy of Janelle Molony.

deeply embarrassed by his mother's committal and her absence from his life as a child. This is evidenced in his writing, as well as in Martha's poems. In addition, Ralph consistently disbelieved that his mother was as crazy as the news articles made her out to be. In his 1987 reminiscence, *A Grandfather Remembers*, Ralph explained that he knew Martha "had some physical problems and an alleged mental condition," though he could not or would not detail either (**see Introduction**).

For the most part, the news reporters wrote with an obvious bias, though no one could prove or disprove Martha's words. Only once in the ninety printings of the tale is there an attempt to get a third party to fact-check the story. The professional opinion a reporter collected came from a St. Paul physician who had treated Martha prior to her going to the insane asylum. This wholly anonymous doctor contributed a singular quote, saying Martha's story is "bunk," with no further explanation (*South Bend Tribune,* 1934, Sept. 20).

The fact that this one doctor had not seen Martha in over six years, should automatically discredit their contribution to her current claims. If he never understood her complaints in the first place, why should readers assume that, after so much time, there would be any change? More suspiciously, though, there is never an inclusion of the capacity in which this doctor had ever treated her, his or her medical specialty, or credentials to speak with authority on the matter. Sadly, the press seemed to have had a field day with this doctor's quote, at Martha's expense.

From this one comment, the articles that followed said that multiple doctors "scoffed," "laughed" and called Martha "derided." In the *Sioux City Journal*, Martha's comment that her condition was "supernatural" was included, but an editor left out her follow-up explanation about feeling cursed because her symptoms defied all available medical treatments, as shown in the earlier articles (1934, Sept. 19, see illustration 40). Then, on September 22, the Ohio *News-Messenger* called living without food Martha's "power," even though Martha clearly spelled out for the interviewer that she was suffering, seeking a cure, and that she found no pleasure or amusement in her circumstances (1934).

Martha's story then caught the attention of the Christian Scientist community who found healing and enlightenment through fasting (primarily Hilton Hotema, but also others who do not necessarily identify as Breatharians). Perhaps, the spiritually themed letters found at the end of Martha's book of poetry were written in response to the news articles (see Letters on the Final

Pages). Though many of the Nasch family knew Martha to be proverbially haunted by her secrets, she was not a spiritually "enlightened" person, despite a religious upbringing. To represent her in this way, would be a mistake. Again, we can point to Martha's direct quote in the *La Crosse Tribune:* "I found a plausible explanation in the Bible" (1934, Sept. 20). Next, she immediately de-emphasizes the value of that find with, "I never paid much attention to the Bible" (**see illustration 46**).

Her disclaimer was supported by her son, Ralph, when he wrote, "My mother never cared much for religion as she thought most people who went to church were hypocrites" (*A Grandfather Remembers*, 1987). He added that "neither of them [his parents] attended church on a regular basis," that even his father "had a 'faith' of his own" and that from it, he was just as qualified for Heaven as any churchgoer (1987).

MONDAY, SEPTEMBER 24, 1934

WOMAN SAYS SHE HAS GONE SEVEN YEARS WITHOUT FOOD

St. Paul, Minn., Sept. 20. — Although doctors scoffed at her story, Mrs. Martha Nasch, 44, a housewife, today reiterated that for seven years she has not eaten, nor drunk, nor slept—and she offered to prove it!

Louis J. Nasch, 50, her husband, said only this:

"I've never seen her eat or drink. That's all I know. I've tried surprises to find her eating, but never have."

Mrs. Nasch interposed:

"I will submit to any test that may be asked if necessary. I will consent to an indefinite constant watch."

Nasch was one of three witnesses to sign Mrs. Nasch's statement concerning her condition. The others are Ralph Nasch, 12, their son, a high school student, and Lynette Claus, 18, a neighbor.

Miss Claus frequently does housework at the Nasch home, and, although she goes in and out all during the day, she has never seen Mrs. Nasch eat or drink, she said.

Mr. Nasch told reporters:

"I do not sleep either. At least not like other people. I seem, rather, to be in a trance—like some one under dental gas. It gives me no rest."

Mrs. Nasch is an excellent cook, although she has no sense of tast, being able to distinguish only between salt and sugar.

Mrs. Nasch was taken to the state hospital at St. Peter when she disclosed her condition to a St. Paul doctor following an operation.

There she claims she ate no food, although continual attempts were made to feed her forcibly.

Mrs. Nasch points to several biblical passages to find an explanation for her condition. She said:

"It says in the Old Testament that 'they shall see food, but not eat.' I don't see why I should be cursed like this, though."

One St. Paul doctor who once had taken care of Mrs. Nasch said:

"I think it's all bunk!"

Illustration 48: Sept. 24, 1934, *Garrett Clipper,* Indiana.

Credit: Associated Press. Accessed through Newspapers.com.

Old Hype Leads Modern Readers to the Truth

Now that we have thoroughly examined the ninety publications, we can pinpoint critical clues to explain Martha's mysterious case of nerves. The answers we have all sought are hidden in plain sight, tucked into the articles for the discerning reader to discover. Because reporters scattered the clues across several versions of the story and framed them to create a sensational narrative, they are easy to miss. In light of this, we will highlight the pertinent clues for the reader, and as we do, we can begin to get a better sense of Martha's habit of making a bold claim followed by a subtle, more truthful, confession. By those confessions, we solve the case.

Truth #1: Martha consumed food during her "fast."

From "Woman Has Gone Without Food, Drink 7 Years," *Sioux City*, Sept. 19, 1934: Martha stated she was concerned by her loss of desire for food, but that eating it did not repulse her.

Truth #2: Symptom onset correlates to Martha's 1927 surgery.

Truth #3: Martha's taste sensation was distorted, not lost.

From "Woman Says She Has Gone Seven Years Without Food," *Garrett Clipper,* Sept. 24, 1934: Martha stated she complained to a St. Paul physician immediately after her June 8, 1927 operation. One complaint was having "no sense of taste" anymore, except for tasting both salt and sugar.

Truth #4: Martha's appetite was not the same as it used to be.

Truth #5: Her complaints prompted a psychiatric evaluation.

From "St. Paul Woman Claims She Hasn't Eaten, Drunk Anything For 7 Years," *LaCrosse Tribune*, Sept. 20, 1934: Martha told her interviewer, "The world was not the same. My body felt and still feels as though it were petrified." She swore, "I could not eat or drink," then clarified, "I did not want [food or drink]." As a result of this postoperative medical consultation, "the doctor told me I had a case of nerves," and a referral to St. Peter's was initiated.

Using these first-person disclosures, readers are forced to consider how Martha's 1927 operation could have caused her strange and chronic symptoms: loss of sensory acuity, reduction of taste sensitivity and flavor discernment, loss or reduction of appetite, weight loss, and the development of food anxiety and comorbid avoidance behaviors (such as hiding and throwing away food while in the asylum, per the *La Crosse Tribune*, Sept. 20, 1934).

Using Martha's direct accounts and modern medical knowledge, we can establish an argument for known medical conditions that correlate to her situation. In this process, we must acknowledge the fact that neither of the authors are medical professionals, only determined researchers. Therefore, we've combed through numerous medical manuals, medical journals, reference books, and recent web articles written by medical professionals in the fields of psychiatry, dentistry, neurology, and more. The full reference list is available at the end of the chapter. We have also consulted with health professionals about the research.

As a final measure, we spoke to several individuals who have personally been affected by the disorder that Martha's clues lead us to. We gave them authority to correct any misunderstandings or misrepresentations of the disorder's effects, prior to book publication. We offer our general gratitude to them, as many requested to remain anonymous.

Moving forward, we will use scientific medical terms related to Martha's case, as defined by the literature we consulted. For the reader's convenience, we will provide a brief explanation of three key terms:

Dysgeusia: The appropriate term for the distortion of one's taste sensation is dysgeusia. This condition differs ageusia, which is the the total loss of taste sensation. (Truth #3 eliminated ageusia as an option.)

Gustatory: The sensory system that controls taste is called gustatory. This system includes functions of the facial nerves, taste buds, saliva production, and tongue movement. (Truth #1 eliminated matters of swallowing or digestion within the stomach or intestine.)

Iatrogenic: An iatrogenic condition is created or caused (*Greek: genic/genesis*) by a physician (*Greek: iatros*). Iatrogenic conditions can result from any medical procedure or application of medical knowledge, the delivery of medication, or by an exam technique. (Truth #2 eliminated gustatory problems as being present prior to Martha's surgery. Rather, they are a secondary condition, or a side-effect, from that physician-directed event.)

In summary, Martha's complaints of dysgeusia, a gustatory disorder, were a complication from the surgery. This is a very important distinction.

What Physician-Directed Events Can Cause Dysguesia?

Iatrogenic taste distortions can be caused in two known ways: through chemical influences or physical trauma to a patient's head or mouth.

We will evaluate both options for Martha's case, eliminating variables, one-by-one, until we reach an irrefutable conclusion. Regarding chemical influences doctors could introduce to a patient, there are "a wide array of medications [that] affect taste function," says Dr. Simpson, "the most frequent complaint being dysgeusia" (*Fundamental Neuroscience for Basic and Clinical Application,* 2018, 334-345). Modern physicians are advised to disclose the possibility of taste loss to all patients who are prescribed such medications that affect the central nervous system, "because of the large number of nerves that relay taste information" (334-345). There is sparse medical research on chemically-induced sensory loss from the 1920s, however, to confirm if doctors back then were aware of the specific side effects of medication on the nervous system.

Some known modern medications that have been linked to dysgeusia are fentanyl, morphine and codeine (opioids), bupivacaine (local anaesthetic), penicillin V potassium (antibiotic), several antihistamines, and many more antipsychotic medications, as inventoried in Drs. Bicknell and Wiggins, "Taste Disorder," article in the *Western Journal of Medicine* (1988, 459). However, back in the 1920's, many of these medications were not in use. Well-known chemical influences introduced in surgeries at that time were ether and chloroform, with the possibility of a post-surgical opiate for pain relief.

If medication, including anesthetics, were the cause of dysgeusia, anticipated side effects would begin shortly after administration then wane within a few months of the patient discontinuing the medication. Even assuming Martha had a brief course of pain relievers after her surgery, in her six months of recovery, the chemically-induced symptoms should have lessened or disappeared entirely. As such, we can rule out chemical influences as a factor in her case because her symptoms persisted.

This ruling forces us to consider what physical forces might have been applied to Martha's head or mouth during her 1927 surgery.

We have found that any tension, torque, tearing, or the crushing of facial nerves can result in the loss of oral sensation and other distortions within the gustatory system. There are two specific facial nerves that might be responsible for Martha's symptoms. We will explore both, but before doing so, we must eliminate any disturbances to facial nerves from a non-surgical impact, such as being hit, thrown, or by falling with head impact.

Dysgeusia has been recorded in medical cases where the temporal bone and proximal nerve bundle are struck (on the side of the skull). Sometimes, when a brain is severely shaken inside the skull, an injury can result in the pons (on the brain stem), on the thalamus (in the center of the brain), or to the midbrain. These areas of the brain host nerves connected to the gustatory system. We can comfortably rule out head trauma prior to Martha's surgery because Martha firmly established the iatrogenic origin of her symptoms in her news interview.

Examples of Iatrogenic Injuries To Facial Nerves

Two *specific facial nerves* have been linked directly to dysgeusia.

First, in a 1995 case study of patients who underwent surgery on their ears, Dr. Henkin reports, "each patient experienced dysgeusia after the procedure, which may [have been] related to surgical manipulation of the Chorda Tympani nerve [accessible] in the middle ear, rather than to effects of anesthesia ("Altered Taste and Smell After Anesthesia," *British Journal of Anesthesia,* 646).

The chorda tympani facial nerve is present near the base of the tongue. It runs underneath the back of the mandible (jaw bone), up and through the temporal bone (from one's temple to just behind their ear). Then, this nerve connects to the ganglion nerve bundle below the base of the skull. This chorda tympani is responsible for communicating taste and touch sensations (including pain and temperature) within the anterior (front) two-thirds of the tongue (Dr. Paul Rea, *Essential Clinically Applied Anatomy of the Peripheral Nervous System in the Head and Neck*, 2016, 21-130).

Second, dental surgeons, Alali and Caminiti, consider the lingual nerve extremely vulnerable to iatrogenic injury because of its superficial access (*OralHealth*, 2018). The lingual nerve operates in a similar fashion to the chorda tympani, though, in addition to registering flavors, this nerve moderates saliva production and controls some motor functions of the tongue. This nerve can be found within the soft palate (underneath the tongue), just underneath one's molar teeth, then it runs the length up inside one's cheek to attach to the facial nerve bundle at the temple (along with the chorda tympani).

Many dental procedures present the risk of "unintentional laceration, crush injury, penetrating trauma, stretch injury [and] chemical insults," to the lingual nerve (Alali & Caminiti, *OralHealth,* 2018). One example of how a surgical patient might be at risk for facial nerve injury is if they are required to keep their mouth opened unnaturally wide. Their facial nerves can be overstretched as a result, which can impact taste sensations, though, "in that case, a gradual recovery after the operation would be expected," say Drs. Bicknell and Wiggins (1988, 459). In Martha's situation, she either never recovered and learned to live with her symptoms, or her recovery time ran much longer than reasonable for this to be her specific trauma origin.

Because the lingual nerve controls a person's salivary functions, when damaged, it is possible for dysgeusia to result from xerostomia: a dry mouth condition where the salivary glands cannot operate as needed for taste buds to thrive (Saboowala, *Dysgeusia,* 2018, 16). Although, as Dr. Saboowala later explains, appropriate levels of bicarbonate ions and glutamate in saliva are necessary to distinguish salty and sweet flavors (11). Since we know Martha could distinguish those two flavors, we will also dismiss this as an origin for her dysgeusia.

Other common oral assaults or dental procedures that pose a high risk of injury or strain to facial nerves include laryngoscopy, tonsillectomy, and direct trauma from tooth extractions (as found in a 2019 case study published in the medical journal, *Maxillofacial Plastic Reconstructive Surgery,* by Drs. Fujita, Mizobata, Nakanishi and Tojyo). Unlike a chemical influence, a traumatic impact would cause immediate symptoms, as fits Martha's story. Nerve damage also comfortably matches the hypoesthesia (loss or reduction of feeling) that Martha described as "petrification."

That being said, we will rule out nerve damage from a dental procedure, in Martha's case, because of strong indications that the surgery was abdominal-gynecological in nature (**see Introduction**). As a reminder to the reader, Martha was too weak to walk, per Louis Jr.'s 1958 records, for (at least) thirteen weeks after the operation (**see illustrations 13, 14, and 26**). This physical weakness does not make sense with a dental procedure. Also, a dental procedure, however complex, would not warrant the level of secrecy the Nasches maintained regarding the original nature of the surgery.

We are left, now, with only one remaining argument for the origin of physical force on Martha's facial nerves during the operation: orotracheal intubation for anaesthesia, with or without a laryngoscope.

How Intubation Causes Nerve Damage

Although over-the-face masks were still in use in the 1920s, especially to assist with bringing a patient to a state of unconsciousness by their own deep breathing, this decade saw a surge of medical developments which provided anaesthesia via nasopharyngeal (through the nose) and intratracheal (through the mouth) methods (Drury, "Anaesthesia in the 1920s," *British Journal of Anaesthesia,* 1998, 102).

The insufflation technique used during the 1920s (blowing medication into the lungs through a catheter) could provide consistent dosing of medication to the unconscious patient (Drury, 1998, 98). As we've previously explored, the chemical substance (ether or chloroform) would not leave Martha with an unusually long-lasting condition, so we are left considering the physical manipulation of the tongue and any pressure applied to either it or to the jaw by the laryngoscope or endotracheal tube (also called "intratracheal"). Either tool could have injured Martha's facial nerves from the force of tube insertion or from pressure created by tool position within the mouth.

In an article on the earliest technology and application of anaesthesia, Dr. Dobell described how physician-surgeons would depress a patient's epiglottis then manually insert a wide bore tube down their throat ("The Origins of Endotracheal Ventilation," *The*

Annals of Thoracic Surgery, 1994, 579). The tube was pushed down through the patient's larynx (vocal chords or voice box) and either slid into the patient's trachea or blocked off the patient's esophagus (579). In the 1920s, there were no dedicated anesthesiologists to perform this task and monitor the administration. Physician-surgeons had to be as efficient and effective as possible, while prioritizing their attention on the surgical operation.

Eventually, a laryngoscope was used to assist with tube insertion, by prying opening the back of a patient's throat to make the process easier. Then, with the advent of a hand or foot pump, the physician-surgeon could manually push air through absorbent material doused with the anesthetic liquids into the catheter that was fed down the patient's throat.

In general, serious injuries from intubation are rare. However, when they occur, the most common damage from a difficult intubation is caused by compression on the lingual nerve, as Dr. Teichner has explained in his research ("Lingual Nerve Injury," *British Journal of Anaesthesia,* 1971, 413). His case study also included nerve damage via compression when oral surgeons used a tongue retractor tool (1971, 413).

Unfortunately, this information was not widely available to medical practitioners of the 1920s. Dr. Teichner found that prior to his 1971 study, "Lingual nerve injury as a complication of laryngoscopy and tracheal intubation appears to be previously undescribed" ("Lingual Nerve Injury," *British Journal of Anaesthesia*, 1971, 413). This explains why it was neither explored or addressed in Martha's case.

A decade later, in 1983, Dr. Edward Loughman confirmed, again, that when a laryngoscope blade puts too much pressure on one side of the tongue, the superficial lingual nerve is impacted ("Lingual Nerve Injury Following Tracheal Intubation," *Anaesthesia and Intensive Care*, 171). While Dr. Teichner's research found recovery times from compression injuries to take from one month to several weeks, by 1983, with access to additional case studies, Dr. Loughman reported that it can take much longer for normal tongue sensations to return. In Dr. Loughman's report, he stated, "in a review of almost three thousand cases of lingual nerve damage ... the majority of cases recover[ed] in six to nine months" (171).

After nearly forty more years of collected data, Drs. Alali and Caminiti have since established the following: "Any damage to the [lingual nerve]," can cause "temporary or permanent general sensory changes" within the mouth (*OralHealth*, 2018). Considering that a lot can change in the field of medical sciences over time, we will briefly summarize key findings from five case studies spanning 1971 to 2019 that are of particular interest to Martha's case.

A Review of Case Studies

In *Teichner's 1971 case study*, one 44-year-old male underwent thoracic surgery where the "direct laryngoscopy was unexpectedly difficult," but the operation continued without issue (413). The patient told his surgeon the day after his procedure, his tongue had "an area of numbness, 'as if it had been injected with Novocaine'" (413). This resonates with Martha's petrified feeling. When the male patient received a neurological examination, he was found to have hypoesthesia on one side of the tongue with dysgeusia. His numbness persisted for three weeks, diminished at five weeks, then resolved in about six months.

Dr. Loughman's 1983 case study included a 39-year-old woman also having a thoracic surgery, where the laryngoscope could enter, but the "orotracheal tube could not be passed" until the patient was given an additional barbiturate and paralytic (1983, 171). Her orotracheal tube passed through on the second attempt. On the first day after her surgery, "she reported persistent numbness of two or three centimetres on the right side of her tongue" (171). In her case, however, she retained her taste appreciation, but full gustatory sensations did not return for six weeks.

In 1995, Dr. Robert Henkin published his case study on fifty-nine patients "with a variety of taste and smell dysfunction complaints that followed a surgical procedure and general anesthesia" (Altered Taste and Smell After Anaesthesia, *Anesthesiology*, 646). In this study, "each patient noted on awakening from anesthesia and regaining composure, including eating and drinking, that a significant alteration in their taste and/or smell function had occurred that encompassed either loss of acuity or distorted function" (646).

In 2014, another case study came out in *Anesthesiology and Pain Medicine*, where total loss of taste sensations (aguesia) were reported in patients after using the style of laryngeal tubes which block the esophagus in the pharynx (Elterman, Mallampati, Kaye, & Urman, 3). The doctors involved in this study, "hypothesized that the etiology was compression of the lingual nerve," and they were seeing familiar recovery times of several months (Elterman, et. al., 3).

Finally, even though we have long since disregarded a dental procedure as Martha's primary reason for surgery, a 2019 case study report from Japan on molar extractions was especially relevant because of one woman's experience. This study featured a 59-year-old woman experiencing a great deal of pain on the left side of her tongue that began after her tooth removal procedure in 2002 (Fujita, Mizobata, Nakanishi & Tojyo, *Maxillofacial,* 2019, 2). For seventeen long years, she regularly complained of pain, anxiety, depression, and a drastic reduction in the quality of her life (4).

This woman was referred to a psychiatrist for treatment of the symptoms with "heavy psychotropic drugs" (4). After modern psychiatry failed to address the issue, this woman sought a corrective microsurgery repair to her lingual nerve. The result of her surgery was the full recovery of her gustatory sensations (4). Her case sounds all too similar to Martha Nasch's, even with ninety years between for new medical science discoveries and data to help physicians pinpoint lingual nerve damage for treatment.

From this last case, we can clearly see how continuous or chronic taste disturbances, left untreated (or ineffectively treated), can lead to significant mental health concerns in those who suffer. The surgeons who completed this 2019 study (Fujita et. al.) concluded the same: "Misdiagnosed [or] conservative treatments for serious lingual nerve injuries can induce the patient to serious mental disability" (1).

For years, studies on taste disorders have pointed to concurrent mental psychoses such as severe mood changes, anxiety, depression, gustatory hallucinations or amnesia, and food-related paranoia "that can easily be mistaken for psychiatric illness," as was declared by Drs. Bicknell and Wiggins ("Taste Disorder," *Western Journal of Medicine* (1988, 458). In one of very few books currently available on the topic of dysgeusia, Dr. Hakim Saboowala listed known psychological impacts of the condition (regardless of cause) as: increased stress, reduced appetite, lethargy, unwanted weight loss, and a depressed immune system (*Dysgeusia: Symptoms, Causes...*, 2018, 37-39).

As we reached the end of the research available to us at the time of publication, we believe we have found the answer to the question, "What was wrong with Martha Nasch?" Additionally, we've definitively shown how dysgeusia symptoms can be experienced as and interpreted as an expression of mental illness, even to this day.

For what it is worth now, we declare Martha Nasch sane.

Chapter References

Alali, Y., Mangat, H., & Caminiti, M. (2019, December 02). Lingual Nerve Injury: Surgical Anatomy and Management. Retrieved July 22, 2021, from https://www.oralhealthgroup.com/features/lingual-nerve-injury-surgical-anatomy-management/

Bicknell, J. M., & Wiggins, R. V. (1988, October). Taste disorder from zinc deficiency after tonsillectomy. *The Western Journal of Medicine, 149(4)*. 457–460. Retrieved from https://www.ncbi.nlm.nih.gov/pmc/articles/PMC1026505/

Dobell, A. R. (1994). The origins of endotracheal ventilation. *The Annals of Thorasic Surgery, 58*(2), 578-584. doi:10.1016/0003-4975(94)92269-1

Drury P. M. (1998). Anaesthesia in the 1920s. *British journal of anaesthesia, 80*(1), 96–103. doi: 10.1093/bja/80.1.96.

Elterman, K. G., Mallampati, S. R., Kaye, A. D., & Urman, R. D. (2014, September 09). Postoperative alterations in taste and smell. In *Anesthesiology and Pain Medicine 4(4)*. doi: 10.5812/aapm.18527

Fasts Seven Years [Editorial]. (1934, September, 25). *Latrobe Bulletin*, p. 4.

Fujita, S., Mizobata, N., Nakanishi, T., & Tojyo, I. (2019, December 23). A case report of a long-term abandoned torn lingual nerve injury repaired by collagen nerve graft induced by lower third molar extraction. *Maxillofacial Plastic Reconstructive Surgery, 41, 60 (2019)*. doi: 10.1186/s40902-019-0243-z

Henkin, R. I. (1995, September 01). Altered Taste and Smell after Anesthesia Cause and Effect? In *Anesthesiology*, 83. 648-649. doi: 10.1097/00000542-199509000-00042

Her 'Seven-Year Fast' Is Derided [Editorial]. (1934, September 25). *Muncie Evening Press*, p. 9.

St. Paul Woman Claims She Hasn't Eaten, Drunk Anything For 7 Years [Editorial]. (1934, September 20). *La Crosse Tribune*, p. 10.

Loughman, E. (1983). Lingual Nerve Injury Following Tracheal Intubation. *Anaesthesia and Intensive Care, 11*(2), 171. doi:10.1177/0310057X8301100216

Miscellany. (1934, October 8). *Time, XXIV*(15).

No Food in 7 Years [Editorial]. (1934, October 1). *Fort Worth Star*, p. 6.

Rea, P. (2016). Head: Chorda Tympani. In *Essential Clinically Applied Anatomy of the Peripheral Nervous System in the Head and Neck*. (pp.21-130). San Diego, CA: Elsevier Science. doi:10.1016/C2014-0-05021-6

Saboowala, H. (2018). *Dysgeusia: Symptoms, causes, diagnosis, and treatment.* Hakim Saboowala.

Simpson, K. L. (2018). Olfaction and Taste: Disorders of the Gustatory System, In Haines, D. E., & Mihailoff, G. A. *Fundamental neuroscience for basic and clinical applications* (5th ed.). (pp. 334-345). Philadelphia, PA: Elsevier. doi:10.1016/B978-0-323-39632-5.12001-8

Seven-Year Faster and Husband [Editorial]. (1934, September, 22). *News-Messenger,* p. 1.

Teichner, R. L. (1971). Lingual Nerve Injury: A Complication of Orotracheal Intubation. *British Journal of Anaesthesia, 43*(4), 413-414. doi:10.1093/bja/43.4.413

"Throw away your diet lists…" [Editorial]. (1934, September 24). *Johnson City Press,* p. 6.

Woman Claims She Has Gone Seven Years Without Food [Editorial]. (1934, September 20). *South Bend Tribune,* p. 4.

Woman Has Gone Without Food, Drink 7 Years [Editorial]. (1934, September 19). *Sioux City Journal,* p. 1.

Woman Says She Has Gone Seven Years Without Food [Editorial]. (1934, September 24). *Garrett Clipper,* p. 3.

Commentary on Martha

Nasch's Poetry

Janelle Molony, M.S.L.

Great-Granddaughter of Martha Nasch.

281

In 1932, my great-grandmother, Martha Nasch, finalized her collection of eighty poems she'd been composing over time while in residency at the St. Peter State Hospital for the Insane. It is entirely probable that she filled out other notebooks before or after this date, though there is no evidence in family possession.

She wrote in a 160-page, marbled blue grade school composition book which she addressed to her sister, Emma, with a note on the first page that reads: "Let me know if you get this book. 1932" (see illustration 50). It is important to note the person of address on the first page of the book. Emma Augusta Wildemere Gruening was Martha's younger sister by eight years (see Family Trees). This note to Emma tells the reader several things: 1) Martha intended for her poetry to be read. 2) Martha intended for certain poems to be delivered or presented to specific individuals. 3) Martha could receive many visitors, or otherwise meet with extended family members while in residency.

The going rate for this common drugstore item in the 1930s was between $.05 - $.10 USD, or the equivalent of $2.00 USD in the year 2021, though it's likely that a family member or hospital staff provided her with the book.

In this executive-sized 10" x 7" book (see illustration 49), Martha wrote on ninety-five pages, twenty-two of which are on the backside (left) pages. Fourteen double-sided blank pages are torn out and missing. She numbered the top right corner of each page front, just as would have been expected for her to do in a school assignment. There are few erasure marks, which suggests earlier drafts being composed on other pages, reserving this book for my great-grandmother's final drafts.

Martha likely composed her poems during her leisure time. Research has confirmed there were several group classes and activities at the hospital to assist with reforming patients and occupying their time with things like handiwork and gardening. There was also a library on campus, which may have provided Martha with dedicated quiet time, the illusion of privacy, and more space to write away from her "hard bench," as described in "The Coat."

Martha's access to a pencil might have been limited to her designated activity time, as another patient has explained. A patient called Jim Curran who spent time at the hospital from 1930 to 1932 and later disclosed that pens and pencils were not available for patients to hang on to, as a matter of safety. A hospital attendant explained to him when relieving him of his personal effects, "of course you would not harm any one else or yourself - but who knows when some really dangerous patient might get ahold" (Krauch, *A Mind Restored,* 1937, 82-83. **Also see Introduction.**).

Illustration 49: The font cover of Martha's blue marbled composition book from St. Peter's State Hospital for the Insane, 1932. She has written both her maiden and married names on the cover.

Credit: Janelle Molony, personal collection.

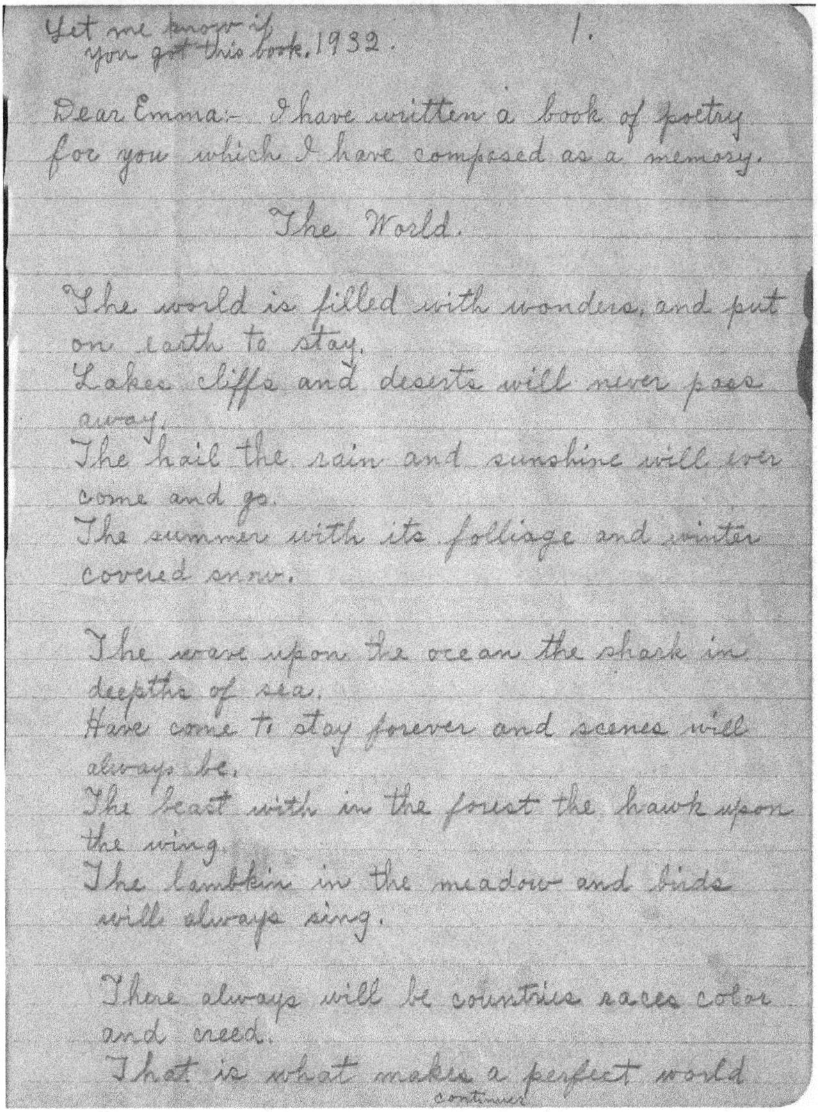

Let me know if
you got this book. 1932.   1.

Dear Emma:— I have written a book of poetry
for you which I have composed as a memory.

The World.

The world is filled with wonders, and put
on earth to stay.
Lakes cliffs and deserts will never pass
away,
The hail the rain and sunshine will ever
come and go.
The summer with its follage and winter
covered snow.

The wave upon the ocean the shark in
deepths of sea,
Have come to stay forever and scenes will
always be.
The beast with in the forest the hawk upon
the wing,
The lambkin in the meadow and birds
will always sing.

There always will be countries races color
and creed.
That is what makes a perfect world
                                                    continued

Illustration 50: The first page of Martha's poetry notebook showing a dedication to Emma, dated 1932.

Credit: Janelle Molony, personal collection.

285

It is probable Martha shared several of her writing samples with other patients, and possibly with staff, as a form of entertainment and to receive feedback. Writing poetry upon request may have earned Martha favors, privileges, or money from those who made the request. In fact, thirty-five of the eighty poems are specifically addressed to individuals.

Though there is no evidence that this story is about Martha, in Jim Curran's account there is a mention of a woman reciting poetry at one of the hospital's social functions. He recalled:

"A woman got up on stage to give a recitation. She wore a dark-blue silk dress, she was stout, and she had light hair, and she was evidently no longer very young. ... She recited a simple little verse ... She looked happy and pleased with herself as she stood on stage. When she had finished, there was loud and long applause. Many of the patients enjoyed the opportunity for making noise. The performer was only too eager to give an encore. Here was an opportunity to show off, and to be of importance for once" (Krauch, *A Mind Restored,* 1937, 167.).

Martha's subject matter varied wildly, from the simplicity of her garden to highly supernatural themes, but her two favorite people to write about were her husband, Louis Nasch Jr., and her only son, Ralph Nasch. Because of the repeated "To" addresses she includes near the top of the page or in the subtitles, it is likely she expected Emma to deliver these poems to the named individuals. This would have been an impractical task, as Martha had composed poems on both the front and back sides of the pages. It may have also been an uncomfortable request that Emma did not comply with, especially since the first poem in the book addressed to Louis Jr. slays him with a bitter "Go jump off a cliff" sentiment.

She wrote on events that occurred from as far back as recounting her own mother's wedding in Germany and immigration to the United States, and as recently as modern-day events that occurred in 1932 which she must have heard about through her visitors. Practically speaking, we can restrict the original dates of Martha's writing between her admission date in 1928 to her opening note showing 1932, though, if other books existed, it could be a more narrow date range.

Her poems are mostly narrative ballads or odes to a particular person or season of life, though many offer rhetoric or allegory. She frequently turns to hyperbole or metaphor to exaggerate her feelings on life's circumstances, especially her living conditions in the asylum, though research into the hospital's history and photographic evidence suggests a more pleasant picture than Martha draws.

In May 1946, *Life* magazine published "Bedlam 1946," an exposé of two American state-run hospitals: Pennsylvania's Byberry and Ohio's Cleveland State. Author Albert Q. Maisel reported, "Court and grand-jury records document scores of deaths of patients following beatings by attendants. Hundreds of instances of abuse, falling just short of manslaughter, are similarly documented ... to be covered up by a tacit conspiracy of mutually protective silence and a code that ostracises employees who sing too loud."

According to Maisel, the patients were fed a "starvation diet," and thousands (per his own observations) spent their days "locked in devices euphemistically called 'restraints': thick leather handcuffs, great canvas camisoles, 'muffs,' 'mitts,' wristlets, locks and straps and restraining sheets. Hundreds are confined in 'lodges'—bare bedless tombs ... by day lit only through half-inch holes through steel-plated windows, by night merely black tombs" (1946).

In my wishful thinking, I hope that my great-grandmother's experience was somehow an exception to this description of horror, though the 1948 exposé in the *Minneapolis Morning Tribune* did not reveal as much. To bank on a more pleasing re-telling of Martha Nasch's experience would be to either fully

288

disregard the direct accounts of patient #20864, or to whitewash her tales as unreliable (coming from a crazy person), and perpetuate a grand scale cover-up.

If she wrote letters home about her condition, they would have been pre-screened by a nurse or social worker in the hospital's office, prior to being stamped (Krauch, *A Mind Restored*, 1937, 98). This censorship helped hospital management to avoid the spread of blasphemous lies or harmful allegations (or slanderous truths which would damage the hospital's reputation). Former patient H.H. Hanley reported to Alice Russell that "patients have little privacy in their correspondence. They can have but one correspondent at a time, and cannot change oftner [sic] than once in three months" (as cited by Russell in *Women of the Asylum*, 1994, 200). Because of this, Martha may have recorded her more risqué eyewitness accounts in poetic form and possibly hidden the notebook to avoid it being read by prying eyes until she could hand-deliver it into a visitor's hands.

One such poem that may have been prevented from release is "Mary." While it does not speak to treatment Martha directly received by any staff of the hospital, it reveals a systemic latency in addressing distressing and even deadly practices.

Martha originally wrote in cursive and with a pencil, though there are noticeable shifts in her handwriting style that are worth mentioning. The first sixty-four poems found in the notebook are composed with what we will call a "functional" cursive, and appear on the numbered, right-hand pages only. Beginning with Martha's sixty-fifth poem, her handwriting and poem formatting suddenly changes. For the remainder of the notebook, Martha writes in a formal script, closely resembling calligraphy (if it could be accomplished with pencil). It is also at this point that Martha started writing on both sides of the pages and the titles of her poems are presented with proper quotation marks.

The most frequently applied poetic structure and rhyme scheme is an 8-6-8-6 quatrain meter (appearing twenty-one times) with an aBcB rhyme scheme (used fifty-five times). When Martha strays from this meter, her signature stamp can still be seen in landing shorter lines on the sixth syllable.

When reading and analyzing her writing style, the monotony of this structure and rhythm became a barrier to seeing and "hearing" the story with fresh eyes. When able and appropriate, I've made adjustments to the visual presentation to maintain interest. Some poems have meter marks intentionally added in to show Martha's attention to this detail. One hypothesis for her signature meter is due to the familiarity of rhythms Martha may have been exposed to at an early age. For example, her second-most used meter (7-6-7-6) is heard in the popular nursery rhyme, "Mary Had a Little Lamb."

If viewed in the original order of composition, one can observe Martha's writing skill developing (**see Appendix for the original order**). Over time, she shows less dependence on conventional punctuation (specifically a comma or period after each line, regardless of it being a sentence or complete clause). She starts to incorporate slant rhymes as needed to get her point across, as well as using invented spellings to accomplish a desired rhyme or meter perfection. These improvements suggest Martha studied poetry in books she could borrow from the hospital's library. Published poets she may have been influenced by at this time include William Shakespeare, Emily Dickinson, Robert Frost, Lewis Carrol, Elizabeth Barrett Browning, and popular hymnist, John Newton.

Martha seems quite aware of her progressing writing talent. Even her own son, Ralph, considered her poems "very good," per his conversations with my mother, Jodi Nasch Decker. In the poem "Rhyme," she teases the reader with the idea that her poetry is more rewarding than any other job.

The average length of Martha's poems is twenty-two lines, which allows for fitting the entire poem on one plus one-half of the lined pages, though the longest fills three full pages. "Life in

Northern Pines," is the longest narrative poem Martha included at sixty-six lines in eight and one-half quatrain stanzas (or seventeen couplets) in an aBcB rhyme scheme. Due to the length, this poem has been arranged in paragraph form to assist with the reading experience. A close second place is "The Asylum," coming in at sixty-four lines and eight stanzas of the same aBcB rhyme scheme. There are seven poems competing to be the shortest, most within a section of her notebook she originally labeled, "Odd Verses and Rhymes." Of the seven, they all are composed of four lines (more reasonably a single couplet) and for argument sake, "Rhyme," is the shortest by word count, at exactly twenty-two words.

Martha wrote 86% of her poems in first-person perspective, including seven that were written from either Ralph or Louis Jr.'s viewpoint. It's clear she includes herself when writing in third-person voice, though less than half of her second-person "you's" can be identified.

The most frequently used words found in her poetry (excluding titles) are organized in the table on the next page. From this table, we can make several conclusions about her overall homesickness and those she missed the most with "little" indicating her child and "dear" used as a pet name for her husband (though not exclusively).

Word	Usage (number of uses)
home	54
life	48
little	38
would	36
dear	36

Word frequency obtained through dataBasic.io after eliminating irrelevant filler words such as "a" and "the."

By indexing the themes and keywords of each poem, we find that Martha's top themes, in quantity of mentions, are "home," "love," "heart," then "children." Curiously, Martha does not write about the medical affliction she claims to have necessitated her confinement.

Though devils, demons, and sin are frequently referenced as points for when or why things in Martha's life turned sour, she also personifies poverty, temptation, and misfortune as generic alternatives to darker spiritual themes. It should also be noted that the combined use of these concepts are still outweighed, at large, by the more endearing themes I previously listed.

A third and final shift in Martha's handwriting is seen in the two final pages, at the back of the composition notebook.

Found there are two letters that are most curious, but insufficiently explained. Both were transcribed and included in the Appendix.

The first letter has the city and state of Winfield, Kansas listed at the top right corner (a college town southeast of Wichita), along with the date of 1935. This would have been received after Martha's early discharge from the hospital in July of 1934, and after her news media interview (**see Epilogue**). It is signed with only a first name: Bethel. The second letter shows a location of Bryn Maur, Washington (just south of Seattle), that is signed from a Theo Bisson and dated October 21, 1934. How she knew of these people, or if she personally knew them, is unknown.

From comparing the handwriting to earlier poems, particularly in the greetings "Dear Mrs. Nasch" and "Mrs. Martha Nasch," we can conclude that Martha, herself, transcribed them with blue ink pen and in exemplary cursive. The presence of *any* post-committal notes indicates that the original book was returned to Martha upon her release (allowing time for her to add the two letters), before it was eventually inherited by son, Ralph, who has since passed the material through to his descendants. The presence of these poems also raises the question of why Martha is transcribing them into her book. Or perhaps, the question should be rephrased as: Why is Martha trying to save the letters into this *particular* book?

Perhaps Martha received solace or support from these outsiders or held similar beliefs or explanations for her condition. The earlier letter writer recommends Martha settle down and rest, while the latter praises and commends her bravery.

Illustration 51: July 10, 1942. "At Highland Park, Martha, 52 years." Louis Jr. tooks these photos of Martha to send to Ralph in California while he trained for the Army Air Force.

Louis wrote, "Ralph left for the War when you inlested [sic] June 13, 1942, 12:30p.m. at the Federal Bilding [sic] Minneapolis, Minnesota. Your Mother and Pa were there to visit you yet before you's all had to leave with the train" (1957).

Credit: Louis Nasch Jr. Courtesy of Ralph Nasch.

One strange inclusion in Theo's letter was that he sent her $1.00 USD with no explanation. In 2021, this equates to $20.00 USD. Ralph Nasch, my grandfather, has shared stories about how Martha would speak about her condition and experience on a local circuit and earn money from sharing her testimony. Theo may have been a fan-follower after seeing her story in a newspaper. He believed Martha gained spiritual power by fasting. He offered to pray for her and begged for more letters from her, "that we may learn more of your wonderful spirituality."

Neither a Bethel nor Theo/Theodore Bisson corresponds to a person in Martha's family tree. We can speculate from the spiritual-religious jargon used in both letters, that they are from Christian Scientists: Bethel being a teacher-guru of sorts, and Theo, an equally strong believer and reinforcer of the dogma which suggests Martha had been spiritually reborn and was now "only 6 ½ years old." These encouraging letters may have impressed a certain sacredness on Martha's experience as a type of reformation and thus increased the importance of the notebook.

If we were to revisit the idea of Martha's experience as an example of the Breatharian lifestyle that emerged from splinter religions or cults of the twentieth century (despite strong evidence against this), then these two letters might be interpreted as zealous validation for Martha's living without food or water long-term as a path to her nirvana. If this were the case, curious and responsible minds should also revisit the pre-death visions my great-grandmother saw which were nowhere close to heavenly.

Illustration 52: June 14, 1942. "At the falls. A picture of your mother."

The falls mentioned might be either Hidden Falls or Minnehaha Falls, along the Mississippi River.

Credit: Louis Nasch Jr. Courtesy of Ralph Nasch.

Appendix

Letters on the Final Pages

To Martha, From Washington

Bryn Maur, Washington

October 21, 1934

Dear Mrs. Nasch:

To say that you have my utmost sympathy for having survived 6 1/2 years of fasting is what we all new you. where having gone so long without nourishment has lowered Your vitality and that accounts for the very gloomy feeling expressed in your letter. I do not believe God had forsaken you. God says, " I shall never forsake thee nor leave thee." the very fact that we breathe assures us of His grace. it is only your lowered Vitality that makes you speak that way. you are now 6 1/2 years old and I shall pray God that you become of age that we may learn more of your wonderful spirituality.

This is your opportunity – I would be very thankful if you remain always cheerful and of good courage. I enclose $1.00. Please do not make much effort to say much. If you delay all effort from writing until you are greatly strengthened, it would please me. Look to God to strengthen your spirituality.

Read little, think less – just feel relaxed in the Lord then shall you be refreshed.

Your friend, Theo Bisson

Post Ofc. address Bryn Maur, Washington

Editorial Comments

This letter was found on the backside of page 72, in Martha's poetry journal. The $1.00 USD is the equivalent of $20.00 in 2021.

To Martha, From Kansas

Winfield, Kansas

March 5, 1935

Mrs. Martha Nasch –

My dear: Your letter and the dear little greeting was surely a great joy, for in your first letter you seemed so sad and downhearted, because of your people not understanding you and in your last letter you had visited them and everything seemed quite harmoniously happy and peaceful. You see, "all things work to for good to them who love the Lord" so that the former things may be forgotten and the "Eternal now" be realized with joy. I had to smile over the part of your letter that illustrated your trip – especially the dance – I am under the impression your husband would have given a sixpence to have seen you and Ralph would have had the greatest fun of all.

To-day the sun is shining –my gas turned down low and the door ajar about 5 inches, the beautiful green grass looks quite spring like and most of the gardens are planted. I have been quite busy since last writing to you, I have three classes Saturdays and two Thursdays. I love the work – my heart and soul are in it, and when I know a class is interested I am in "The Seventh Heaven" teaching them and helping them – and helping them to get the Understanding. I have also given Astronomical readings – so many people have what they call their good days and their bad days, not realizing that through the power of the mind, the bad days can be converted into good days – I sometimes think some people are mentally lazy – They prefer being *intertained* to learning how to help themselves – Of course it takes a study of years to learn but I truly think it is worthwhile a million times over.

I think it lovely of Ralph to attend the Bible class and it is only a few weeks till Palm Sunday. I surely thank you for the invitation to visit you should I go to St Paul – and also for your kind wish for me for "Health happiness and success."

I have your last drawing before me – it is so dear and as I see the tinted clouds I think of the many beautiful sunsets I can see from my West window – sometimes the sun – when setting or rather as we see it last at night looks like a large ball of fire or gold, as it is being hid from view by the horizon.

I am glad you were so happy in your last letter. Keep on being happy dearie – for happiness brings joy – love – and peace –

God forever Bless you and your loved ones.

Lovingly

Bethel

Editorial Comments

This letter was found on the from and back of page 73, in Martha's poetry journal. Bethel references English money ("sixpence").

Illustration Index

Poem Index

Please be advised:
Items are indexed by poem number, not page number.

12, 13, 14, 31, 36, 39,
54, 56, 61, 66, 73, 74,
76, 77, 78

Follow

17, 33, 42, 71

Forget/Forgotten/Bygone

1, 5, 8, 10, 11, 14, 16,
17, 18, 29, 31, 40, 43,
69, 75, 79

Forgive/Forgiveness

7, 42, 80

Friend

2, 8, 17, 26, 37, 40, 43,
58, 60, 62, 63, 64, 66,
68, 69, 77, 79

God/God's Will

1, 3, 5, 8, 11, 12, 22, 23,
31, 34, 40, 43, 45, 46,
49, 54, 56, 66, 70, 75,
79, 80

Grief/Sorrow

5, 6, 7, 8, 20, 40, 69,
70,

75

Heaped

20, 21, 23, 36, 75, 76

Heart

1, 2, 5, 6, 7, 8, 9, 10,
11, 15, 16, 21, 26, 27,
30, 37, 42, 51, 53, 59,
61, 64, 68, 69, 70, 75

Home/Cottage

1, 2, 5, 7, 10, 12, 13,
16, 17, 19, 20, 21, 22,
23, 25, 31, 32, 34, 35,
37, 38, 39, 40, 44, 45,
47, 51, 57, 59, 62, 65,
67, 69, 70, 71, 79

Illness/Sickness/Medical Care

43, 49, 70, 71

Jesus

33, 36, 42, 56, 59, 61,
69, 76, 80

Joy/Happiness/Cheer

Original Poem Order

1. The World
2. A Painter
3. Forgotten
4. Broken Romance
5. Forsaken
6. Suffering
7. The Vacant Chair
8. Unfaithful
9. Sympathy
10. In Memory
11. A Mother Gone
12. Mother's ways
13. Perfect Dad
14. Ralph
15. Our Mamma
16. A Scene From Beyond
17. A Bed
18. Disappointment
19. Untitled
20. The Blue For-Get-Me-Not
21. Flowers
22. A Bride
23. Son In Need
24. Somewhere
25. Advized By Dad
26. Ballad Of Louis
27. An Old Fashion Dwelling
28. Unhappy Home
29. Happy Home
30. Lake Pleasures
31. A Friend
32. Dearest Friend
33. A Cottonwood Tree
34. Courtship Days
35. Pretty Boy
36. Babe O-Mine

Thank you for reading this book!

For more books by Janelle Molony, please check out the projects below and her author website at **www.JanelleMolony.com**

Seven Years Insane   (fiction, in development)
Social Media @SevenYearsInsane

When the entire country has fallen into the worst economic depression of its time, Martha Nasch faces the greatest betrayal of her life. Her pleas for help only bring scoffing from those she thought she could trust. Locked away in a state asylum, she must endure the consequences of her cheating husband's choice, if she ever wants to see her son again. No one would believe a crazy woman's story, now, would they?

From Where I Sat   (fiction, in development)
Social Media @RousseauProject

Escaping the Civil War is extra hard when one's family is tied up in political schemes. To avoid the next round of drafts, a grand plan brings four families from Pella, Iowa together for the greatest adventure of their lives on the Overland-California trail. Between the endless starry nights and daytime gunfights with menacing Indians, Mrs. Sarah Rousseau logs the wagon train's progress in her pocket diary. As a wheelchair-bound woman, she's not able to help when supplies run low and desperate choices must be made before they reach the snow-covered Sierra Nevadas standing between them and their California dreams. All she can do is write down what happens next.

Now on sale!

Un-Adoptable? Faith Beyond Foster Care (non-fiction, on sale now)

Website JanelleMolony.com/AdoptionToLife
Social Media @AdoptionToLife

When an adoptive mother is presented with a foster child that doesn't fit the description, quick-thinking helps her navigate a situation that was set up to fail. Faced with either turning her back on the child or turning to God for help, she fights for what she believes to be right.

Awards and Recognition: Amazon Bestseller 2020, National Indie Excellence Award Finalist 2020, Readers' Favorite 5-Star Rating, Arizona Authors Association 2020 Literary Contest Winner, Perfect Score from Writer's Digest Self-Published Book Awards.

Now in paperback, e-book, and audiobook!

Finally, an honest review of your reading

experience is highly appreciated!

Please share your opinions on this book with the

location of your purchase and on social media.

To inquire of the research and writing team,

send a message through www.JanelleMolony.com/contact

CPSIA information can be obtained
at www.ICGtesting.com
Printed in the USA
LVHW081636270322
714519LV00012B/1247

9 781088 017630